AF679191

INDUSTRIAL ORGANISATION AND ENTREPRENEURSHIP

INDUSTRIAL ORGANISATION AND ENTREPRENEURSHIP

R. Jayaprakash Reddy
M.Com., M.Phil., Ph.D.

A P H PUBLISHING CORPORATION
ANSARI ROAD, DARYA GANJ
NEW DELHI-110 002

Published by
S.B. Nangia
A.P.H. Publishing Corporation
4435–36/7, Ansari Road, Darya Ganj,
New Delhi-110002
Phone: 011–23274050
e-mail: aphbooks@gmail.com

2026

© Reserved

Rs. 2495/-

Typeset by
Ideal Publishing Solutions
C-90, J.D. Cambridge School,
West Vinod Nagar, Delhi-110092

Printed at
RD DIGITAL PRINTERS
Ansari road , Daryaganj, Delhi-110002

SYLLABUS COVERED

- **Industrialisation** - Meaning: Rationale : Factors hampering Industrial Development in India.
- **Interdependence of Agriculture and Industry** - Their terms of trade.
- **Concept of Optimum firm** - Factors Determining Optimum size of the firm - Measures of size of a firm - Recent trends in the size of Indian industries.
- **Theories of Industrial Location** - A critical appraisal.
- Finance of Industry - Recent trends in Money Market and Capital Market.
- **Joint sector** - Formation Joint Sector Enterprises: Rationale of Joint Sectors Evolution of Government Policy -The Concept of National Sector.
- **Stock Exchange and Its Regulation** - Meaning. Importance and Functions: Organisation and Regulation of Stock Exchanges, Securities Contracts (Regulation) Act - Recent Amendments to SCRA.
- **Industrial Policies** - Industrial Policy Resolutions of 1948 and 1956 - Appraisal of Industrial Policy Statements of 1970, 1977,1980,1990 and 1991.
- **Industrial Licensing Policy and Regulation of Industry** - Regulation of Concentration of Economic Power - Control of Monopolistic and Restrictive Trade Practices - Regulation of Foreign Private Investments and collaboration Agreements.
- **Entrepreneurship** - Concepts Objectives and significances. Theories of Entrepreneurship.
- **Entrepreneurship and Economic Development** - Relevance to Society, Entrepreneurial attitude. Motivation and Personality.
- Programmes and Policies for promoting Industrial Entrepreneurship.

PREFACE

In commerce there are many textbooks and guides available to the students both at under graduation and post graduation levels. However, for students who can spare less time and want to get maximum benefit some notes like material consisting of questions and answers is required. Keeping this in view, study material for certain papers has been prepared for B.Com and M.Com students after consulting various standard textbooks and related magazines. Based on the given syllabus some selected questions are answered at the examination point of view. Though the questions are less in number they almost cover the syllabus. Further, they are answered in simple English. Students are advised to go through this material before the examinations to save time and to score reasonably good marks.

Regular students who go through standard textbooks can also utilize this material and save the time of preparing separate notes. As and when the question needs required figures, diagrams, problems are given for clarity and easy understanding. If answers are discussed at length they loose the said purpose. That is why the answers are given in simple are shorter form suitable for the examinations. Students are further advised to present the answers given in full without any deletion.

The students and the teachers are requested to send their valuable suggestions if any for the improvement of the material. I am thankful to the A.P.H. Publishing Corporation, New Delhi for bringing this material into light.

R. Jayaprakash Reddy

CONTENTS

1. INTERDEPENDENCE OF AGRICULTURE AND INDUSTRY

It is unreal to say that agricultural development and industrialisation are different or competitive. Particularly in underdeveloped countries where agricultural production is less, there would not be any competition between agriculture and Industrial sector. Besides, these two have interrelation, increase in agricultural products is the basis for industrial development.

In the words of Kuznets 'agricultural revolution - a marked rise in productivity per worker in agriculture - Is a precondition of the industrial revolution in any part of the world'. Though there are many advantages through industrialisation, it requires strong agricultural base. In under developed countries, if the agriculture is not modernised the purchasing power of the people goes down which results in slow progress in industrial expansion. In the same manner, if the agriculture sector does not get modernised tools and technical know-how from industrial development, the agricultural development cannot run for a long time. Industrial sector also absorbs human resources from agriculture sector.

The Government's help to one sector may have affect on the other in the short run and it may be a competition. But in the long run, which is more important, there will be good interrelation between these two sectors. If we can verify the financial history of developed countries, it can be known that development in agriculture sector helped for regular increase and development of industrialisation.

The countries at present which are advanced in industrial front were once agriculturally in better position. Historians after careful study came to know that growth and extension of agriculture is the base for industrial establishment and Increase in production. They also observed that though the societies is subject to various changes, the agriculture and industries are interdependent. Any agriculturally developed country can not continue Its financial transactions and develop unless, the agricultural development exists.

Agricultural growth rate and human resource development help for industrial betterment. By diverting rural savings towards investment in industries may be useful for urban development. It is very Interesting to know the analysis, that the influence of industrialisation is on agricultural production and, income. Through intensive cultivation, with the help of industrialisation agricultural production can be increased. In countries where intensive cultivation is difficult due to pressure on land, industrialisation will have preference than agriculture. There Is always interrelationship between low agricultural productivity and Industrial backwardness. Because of this good interrelationship, countries like America and Russia developed both Industrially and agriculturally. The process of industrial development increases the demand for raw materials and food products. Due to purchase of agricultural products by industrial workers, their prices will rise. If the agriculturists sell their products with the increased prices, their financial status automatically increases. It may also lead to increase in production, transport and communication development storage of agricultural produce etc. In this way there is possibility for the development of both agriculture and Industry.

Agriculture sector serves the industry in the following ways:

1. It provides the necessary food to the urban people.
2. It not only creates market to the goods produced through real incomes but also become the base for foreign

income to the industry to buy the necessary capital goods.

3. Because the capital is accumulated through persons, it provides the necessary capital to the industry.
4. Industry with sufficient funds can improve its managerial efficiency.

In this manner agriculture helps in the Increase of industry and production. For financial progress and constructive equilibrium, there must be equal production to that of agricultural Increase. Uncontrollable growth in Industrial sector without changes in agriculture sector leads to inflation, Increase of towns, problem of balance of payments etc. This again leads to worsening of financial position in the long run.

In the opinion of Prof. Rostow, the agricultural products are the important working capital for industrialisation.

It is impossible to separate industrialisation from economic development. It is the result of higher income people who spend much of their income on produced goods and services. And spend only less share on food. By absorbing excess population in rural areas, industry is helping in increasing the efficiency of agriculture.

If we think by keeping long run in view, we can say that both agricultural development and industrialisation are inter related and inseparable.

2. CHARACTERISTICS OF UNDERDEVELOPED COUNTRIES

Countries in the world are divided into developed and under developed or backward or developing countries. Before going to know about the characteristics of under developed countries, it is necessary to know the meaning of the concept.

DEFINITIONS

Some united nations' experts define an under developed country as one in which "on the whole production is carried on with a relatively small of real capital per head and with relatively backward techniques in the broadest sense of the world".

Eugene Stanely defines an under developed country as, "a country characterised by mass poverty which is chronic and not the result of some temporary misfortune, and by obsolete methods of production and social organisation which means that the poverty is not entirely due to poor natural resources and hence could presumably be lessened by methods already proved in other countries".

E. M. Bernstein defines an under developed country in the following lines. " The best test of an under developed country is its level of real Income and the rate at which per capita real income is Increasing. In short, an under developed country is one in which output per capita is relatively low and in which productive efficiency is Increasing very slowly, if at all".

From the above definitions we can say that countries with low real per capita income, chronic mass poverty, poor natural resources, backward techniques and low productive efficiency are called under developed. We can say that countries like America, Britain, Japan etc. are developed and countries like India, Bangladesh, Pakistan etc. are under developed.

CHARACTERISTICS

The following were the characteristics of under developed countries which were accepted by majority of the people.

Low per capita income

In under developed countries most of the people were poor. They would not have sufficient food to eat, proper place to live and reasonable clothes to wear. As per the report of the world bank (1989), the per capita income of majority (56%) people in the world is less than 480 dollars. It shows the difference between developed and under developed countries very clearly.

Much dependence on agriculture

Nearly 70 to 90 percent of the people in under developed countries were living mainly on agriculture. In countries like America and Canada only 5 per cent of the people are depending on agriculture. Besides, the land holdings in under developed countries were less due to population growth. This is the main reason for low yield and productivity.

Population explosion

Over population was the main characteristic of these countries. If we can take the example of our country the present population as per 1991 census is expected around 86 crore, this was only around 40 crore before independence. In the same way, the number *of* persons depending on others income was also high in these countries. By the year 1986 the average life period per head in developed countries was about 76 years, where as in under developed countries it was only 61 years. Over population in these countries leads to low standard of living and many economic and social problems.

Under-utilisation of natural resources

Under developed countries have special characteristic in utilisation of their natural resources. Proper utilisation of natural resources in any country results in economic development. But under developed countries were not utilising their natural resources properly. In the opinion of economists, many countries were under utilising or even wasting their natural resources. These countries were not having the capacity to extract and use the natural resources for economic activities.

Scarcity of capital

These countries always face the problem of capital. The interested entrepreneurs face this problem for establishing industries. The reason for low capital formation in these countries was low saving capacity of the people, Though there were some people who have saving capacity, show interest in buying gold and land instead of investing in industries. Hence the industries face capital scarcity. The savings in the national income was 30 per cent in developed countries. But in under developed countries it was less than 15 per cent.

Low level of industrialisation

Low level of industrialisation was one among the characteristics of under developed countries. Low scientific and technical knowledge, lack of interest on entrepreneurship, less sources of energy etc., were the reasons for this. Lack of proper machinery and spare parts were also the reasons for slow industrialisation. Hence they remain as raw material exporting countries. Besides, they use the limited resources for the production of consumer goods instead of capital goods. Because of heavy investment, long duration for starting the production, low return, the entrepreneurs were not showing interesting for establishing capital goods Industries. This results in slow industrialisation.

Lack of initiative and courage

Though there were sufficient natural resources, some countries were still under developed because of lack of initiative, courage and entrepreneurial ability among the people for establishment of industries. Only some sections of the people were having these entrepreneurial skills. Customs, traditions, blind beliefs etc., were the obstacles for entering into industrial sector in many countries.

Technical backwardness

Lack of scientific knowledge, non-availability of skilled labour, usage of primitive methods and old machines made these countries under developed. They would not spend much on development. They show interest in importing Technical know how instead of developing it in the countries.

Dependence on import Trade

These countries depend much on import trade. They export food and raw materials and import machinery.

Change of profession

In under developed countries, generally people would not change their profession or place due to prevailing social conditions. They want to live on the same profession though there were many problems.

Difference in conditions

There would be large difference between rich and the poor in under developed countries. While towns and cities have modern facilities, villages suffer from the minimum facilities, while industrial sector is ready to adopt modern machines and technical know how, the agricultural sector is depending on primitive methods.

Vicious Circle of Poverty

The under developed countries were in vicious circle of poverty. Nurkse propounded this concept, low productivity lead to low income, low income lead to low savings, low savings lead to low investment, low investment lead to capital scarcity which again lead to low productivity. The vicious of poverty can also be shown as follows.

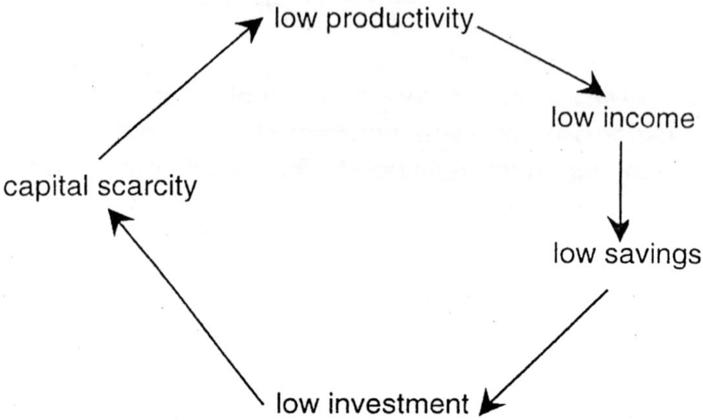

Absence of Women's role in development

Though the women population in under developed countries is equal to men, their importance in economic, special and political activities is very less. And they lead their lives as house wives. But in developed countries, the women are educated and do jobs. The number of literate women in under developed countries is not only less but also play less important role in any sector.

3. FACTORS INHIBITING INDUSTRIALISATION

We have discussed about the characteristics of under developed countries in the above pages. It is very clear that due to industrial backwardness those countries remain underdeveloped. Industrial development leads to increase in income and better of standard of living.

These under developed or developing countries are facing many problems in developing the industries. There were differences of opinions regarding the problems of speedy industrialisation since a long time. That may be the reason why people call 'six economists seven opinions. In the view of Adam Smith, lack of right institutional frame work is the reason for industrial backwardness. Some economists opine that low level of technical know how is the hurdle for industrial development. Some others feel that low level of capital formation and scarcity of natural resources are the main reasons for slow industrialisation. Some more are in the opinion that the population growth is the main hurdle for industrialisation.

Many of the economists are in the opinion that the above said one or more reasons are hindrances for industrialisation. Because of the interrelation among them, it became vicious circle and each problem is playing its role in creating hurdles for industrialisation. We can study about the factors Inhibiting industrialisation in the following lines.

UNDER UTILISATION OF NATURAL RESOURCES

It is impossible to start big industries without sufficient natural resources. Raw materials can be imported but in depression. It is very dangerous. It also depends on the relation with the country supplying raw materials. It is also difficult to Import perishable and heavy weight materials. Besides, the import duty is also high.

Abundant natural resources in a country help for speedy industrialisation. But there should be proper utilisation of these resources. In many developing nations the industrialisation development rate is very less. The reason for this, is not the scarcity but under utilisation of natural resources.

LOW CAPITAL FORMATION

In many developing nations, the capital would not be in the ratio of population and natural resources. The per capita income and the real per capita income of these countries are very less. This low real income will create a 'Vicious Circle'. The following figure shows how low real income leads to low real income again.

Vicious Circle of Poverty

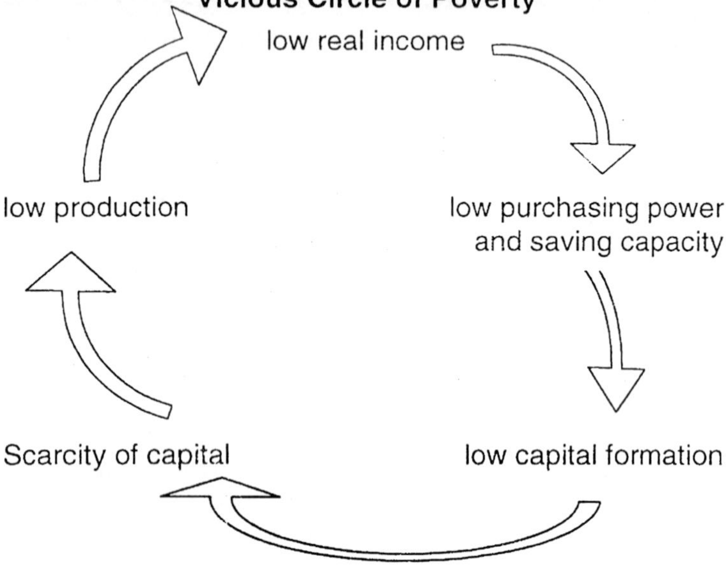

From the above figure it can be seen how the low real income creates low real income again. For industrial development of a nation this vicious circle should be delinked some where or the other. Though it is not desirable to depend on foreign investment, in the initial stages it is better to get foreign aid to delink (break) this vicious circle.

LOW LEVEL OF TECHNICAL KNOWLEDGE

For speedy industrialisation of developing countries Modern technical know how is a must. In the opinion of many economists this is the primary base. Developing nations are backward in technological front. Another problem of these nations is unemployment which is the result of our population. To provide employment to the rural and urban masses these nations give preference for labour oriented industries. In developed nations preference will be given to capital oriented industries. Researches explain that the productivity through mechanisation is more than the productivity through labour. But in developing nations, mechanisation is not possible due to low capital formation. Therefore, it is necessary to mechanise productive policy and to give training to the people in machinery skills for industrialisation of these nations.

POPULATION GROWTH

It is observed that in many of the developing countries the density of population and the growth rate are high. This leads to unemployment. Which does not mean that there is no unemployment in developed countries. But there is difference in nature and volume. Therefore, these countries are bound to show interest on labour oriented industries to solve unemployment problem. This results in low productivity.

BASIC FACILITIES

For speedy industrialisation, the basic or primary facilities like transportation, electricity, communication, water, sheds etc. are necessary. These facilities encourage industrial development. But the developing nations are not in a position to provide them.

POLITICAL INSTABILITY

Absence of political stability affects the industrial productivity. Political stability is more important particularly in the initial stages.

SOCIAL ATTITUDES

Social attitudes of the public also show influence on industrialisation. Peoples energy, efficiency and wants may also help for industrial development. For example, people of Russia and Japan follow punctuality, work regularly and sincerely. These types of attitudes cannot be found in developing countries. Unless these kinds of social attitudes and revolutions occur in the minds of the people, it is difficult for these nations to register rapid industrialisation.

4. OPTIMUM FIRM

Size constitutes one of the important elements determining efficiency of an industrial unit. Economists are concerned with the best size of a producing unit, viz, the optimum scale both of a firm and of an industry. Here we will consider about the optimum firm.

DEFINITION

EAG Robinson defined an optimum firm as follows:

"A firm in which in the existing conditions of technique and organising ability it has the lowest average cost of production per unit, when all those costs which must be covered in the long run are included".

As per the above definition, for determining the optimum size of a firm some conditions are to be fulfilled. They are:

1. conditions of technique and the organising ability to be the same. Any possible changes in the future with regard to the techniques of production and organising ability may affect the optimum level and hence, only existing techniques of production and organisation ability should be taken into consideration.
2. the period must be long run, and
3. existence of perfect competition.

In the present day industrial world firms are not satisfying with the minimum size. They want to increase their size to get the benefits of large scale production. But the firms are going on increasing their size, after a particular stage financial problems will start. That stage can be called as optimum stage or level. Firm functioning at that stage are called 'Optimum firm'.

DETERMINANTS OF OPTIMUM SIZE

EAG Robinson divided the forces which determine the optimum size of all industrial units into five main categories. They are :

1. Technical forces
2. Managerial forces
3. Financial forces
4. Marketing forces
5. Risk and fluctuation forces

Technical Forces

We can not say small size of the firm or big size of the firm is technically optimum. But in some firms to introduce technical forces there must be big Industrial processes. In some cases the firm with small size may work efficiently. But big size firms may work more efficiently. Then increase of size will be favourable. While thinking about technical size, Robinson showed the following factors and the way in which optimum size can be achieved. They are: Division of Labour, absorption of productive process, division of productive activities, usage of big machine, equilibrium of productive processes and getting benefits out of stock. Among these factors, division of labour and usage of machinery are important. By increasing the size production will increase. Many machines may be used to increase the production. There are many advantages in large scale production. For example, by producing double decker buses production is said to be increased by using the technical knowledge.

The optimum size may not be same for all industries. For firms working with big machines, technical department must be big in size. *Ex:* ship building. For producing small products which need less technical skill, optimum technical size is not necessary. *Ex :* Manufacturing of biscuits. In this way we can show the technical optimization in firms.

Managerial Forces

Division of labour and absorption show influence not only in technical department but also in management. In management, there may be many problems since inception of the firm. So, to settle all these problems manager requires high managerial force. A single manager cannot concentrate on all aspects. Hence division of labour is required. In big firms, managerial activities are being looked by directors, chief executive and departmental heads. This managerial division is of line, line and staff and functional organisations.

The size regarding managerial aspect must be optimum. If the size of the firm is big, co-ordination problem will arise. If the size increases at a stage, the average cost of production increases. That is why the average cost of production curve (which means reduction in cost to some extent and its increase afterwards) is in 'U' shape.

In the present circumstances, the industrial aspects like tastes of consumers, expenses of machinery, industrial relations, entry of alternative goods etc., are going on changing. Due to these changes the technical policies will also change. Hence, managerial optimum is required to solve the problems. To control the expenses and to solve the problems efficient management is required. For this purpose managerial optimum is a must.

Financial Forces

Cost of production of a firm depends not only on the technical knowledge of a producer and efficiency of the managers but also on finance which is required for its activities. For some firms like Railways, Electricity. Motor cars, Aeroplanes etc., require, heavy investment even at the time of their establishment. Such organisations may not have problems in collecting the finance. Some times partnership firms may be converted to companies. Such organisations will face financial problems. In this aspect big firms are in advantageous position. But the big firms have risk. Here the important point to be remembered is, the financial forces cannot prescribe the minimum or maximum size. "To understand the real size of the firms in the changing world, financial limitations are also not less important than other aspects.

Marketing Forces

A firm's success depends on its marketing efficiency. Generally, the cost of raw material, which varies from industry to industry, forms a large part in the total cost of the product. Hence the efficient buying of raw materials may make as much difference to final profits as efficient manufacturing. A large firm can affect large scale purchases of raw-materials and enjoy the benefit of lower prices and better selection. A large firm when compared to a small firm will be in a stronger bargaining position with its suppliers. But, a large firm is likely to loose heavily when its expert buyer makes a wrong decision. As the optimum marketing unit is the result of the economies and diseconomies of large scale buying and selling, we have to see what advantages a large firm can derive on the sales side also. By minimising the benefits out of economic buying, marketing optimum can be achieved.

Risk Forces

The risk discourages the growth of firms and earning of profits. This is the big hurdle for firm's growth.

There may be many changes in the demand of the product. If the production made increase with out considering the demand, losses may occur. While thinking of increasing the size of the firm, the present and future demand of the product should be kept in mind.

The changes in demand may be permanent, cyclical, seasonal and erratic. When the tastes of consumers change, the demand for the product changes permanently. The purchasing capacity of the consumer reduces In depression. Firm should reduce its production and costs in this period. But it is not possible to reduce the fixed cost. In such circumstances, the firm may get losses. Some times firm may get loss due to change in the demand of the product. The reasons for such change in demand cannot be known.

The firms are said to be optimum, if they can digest easily the changes in their products' demand. If the producers behave jointly, they can face the risk even in case of severe changes in the demand. This is possible, if some firms join together. Firm producing different products, can reduce its risk by depending on such products which have demand. In this way also firms' optimum size can be identified.

5. THEORIES OF INDUSTRIAL LOCATION

Besides other sectors. Industrial development is necessary for human development. It is not unreal to say that, any country's development mainly depends on industrial development. There are many points to be considered while establishing these important industries. Among the various points, the important aspect is where to start an industry? In olden days location of an industry was not a problem at all. But recently its importance has grown. In the year 1909, Alfred Weber, a German economist framed an elaborated theory on industrial location.

WEBER'S THEORY OF LOCATION

Webar's theory of location is purely deductive in its approach. It says the differences of production costs due to differences in regions is the main reason for industrial location - Weber's analysis is based on general principles which are having an influential bearing on the location of industries and to pull their location to different geographical regions and factors that decide the actual setting up of an industry in a particular locality.

Weber showed two causes for industrial location. They are:

1. Primary causes
2. Secondary causes

Primary causes

These are regional factors to establish industries at a particular region. Other factors like land and buildings, plant and machinery, depreciation, interest etc. does not show influence in industrial location. Industries are pulled towards centres of least transport costs. Lowest transportation costs show influence both on place of consumption and the place of deposits of materials.

Regional Factors

It is natural to change the costs depending on the region. In view of industrial location, difference in different regions can be found. Preference should be given to those costs which can change according to change in region. After careful consideration, Weber identified transportation costs and labour costs.

Transportation Costs

These transportation costs depend on the *weight to be transported* and the *distance to be covered.* For the sake of industries raw material are mainly transported. And finished products should also be transported to market. Because of these reasons Weber Identified transportation costs as an important aspect In industrial location.

All the raw materials useful for an Industry may not be the same. Besides, all types of materials may not be available at all places. Weber classified raw materials into two categories. They are:

i) ubiquities ii) localised materials

i) Ubiquities

These are the raw materials available practically every where.

Ex : brick-clay. Water etc. They would not have any Influence on location.

ii) Localised material

These are the raw materials available only in certain places.

Ex : Iron-ore, minerals, coal, bamboo, wood etc.

They play an important role on the industry than the ubiquities. Depending on the nature of the transformation of materials into products, Weber again categorised raw materials into pure and weight losing.

a) Pure materials

These materials does not lose their weight in production process and appears in the finished product. **Ex:** Iron, cotton, plastic etc.

Industries which use pure materials can locate either near the raw materials centre or near the market. Because there would not be must difference in transportation costs.

b) Weight losing materials

These materials lose their weight significantly and some even lose their identity in the process of production.

Ex : Coal, Sugar cane.

Industries which use weight losing materials should be located near the raw material centres to avoid transportation costs.

Material index

Weber is of the view that the extent to which localised materials impart their weight to the final product is the Governing factor on location of industry. The proportion of the weight of localised material to the weight of the product is known as 'material index' of an industry.

$$\text{Material index} = \frac{\text{Weight of localised material}}{\text{Weight of the product}}$$

If the material index is more than one, it is advised to locate the industry near the raw material centre. And if it is less than one, industry should be located near the consumption centre.

Labour costs

Labour costs, to some extent, may also show influence on Industrial location. The industry is attracted towards lees labour costs. The propensity of labour location to attract the location of an industry is dependent on two Important factors. They are 'labour index' and 'locational weight'. They can be calculated as follows:

$$\text{labour index} = \frac{\text{amount of labour costs}}{\text{labour costs per ton}}$$

Locational Weight = Total weight per unit to be transported

The relation between these two ratios is called 'Co-efficient of labour'. The higher the co-efficient the greater is the tendency for labour locations. The Co-efficient of labour is useful to identify the different stages in labour costs.

Secondary Causes

Weber gave less preference to secondary causes. He divided then Into agglomerative and deglomerative factors. An agglomerative factor is an advantage or a cheapening of production or marketing which results from the fact that production is carried on to some considerable extent at one place. Deglomerative factor is a cheapening of production which results from the decentralisation of production.

Criticism

Techniques of WEber were severely criticised by Sargant Florence, Andreas Predohl, S.R. Dennison and Autin Robinson on the following grounds:

1. Sargant Florence criticised Weber's theory, as it has not considered non-economic aspects viz, historical and social forces.
2. Andreas Predohl criticised Weber's theory on the ground that the distinction between primary and secondary causes is artificial, illogical and arbitrary.
3. Austin Robinson criticised Weber's theory on two aspects. One, in his opinion the assumption of fixed points of consumption does not seem well in a competitive market, two, classification of raw materials into 'Ubiquities' and 'localised' is considered artificial.
4. Dennison criticised Weber's theory on the line that it is over burdened with technical considerations.

Alfred Weber's deductive theory on location, in spite of the shortcomings, is the only theory which has been enjoying the universal acceptance and application.

6. SARGANT FLORENCE'S THEORY

Professor Sargant Florence enunciated location theory based on inductive approach. He criticised Weber's geographical aspect of location. He observed that the relation of an Industry to an area is not so important as the relation of the industry to the distribution of the occupied population as a whole. He makes use of two new concepts viz, 'location factor' and 'co-efficient of localisation' in his theory to explain the existing locational pattern of an industry.

LOCATION FACTORY

It refers to an index of the degree of concentration of an industry in a particular region. Which means, the special attraction to an industry at a particular place can be explained through location factor. The index is calculated by taking two ratios. First, it is the ratio between the workers of the Industry and workers in the region. Second, it is the ratio between workers in the region and workers in the nation. The *first* one is to be divided by the *second* one to find out location factor. If the quotient is one, the location factor is fold to be unity. Which means the industry is evenly distributed through out the country. If the location factor is above unity the region is supposed to have a higher share of the industry than what is legitimately due to it. On the other hand, if it is below unity the region is not supposed to have sufficient share of the industry.

CO-EFFICIENT OF LOCALISATION

Coefficient of localisation is meant to ascertain the propensity of an industry for concentration. It Indicates an Industry's tendency for location anywhere in the country. It is primarily concerned with a particular industry and not a particular region. It will thus be a single figure for the industry and also for the country as a whole. Coefficient of localisation can be found with the help of the following formula.

i) percentage of all workers found in each region,
ii) percentage of workers of industry in question in each region,
iii) positive deviations of ii) from i) are to be added
iv) sum thus derived is to be divided by 100.

On the basis of coefficients it becomes possible to divide the Industries into three categories namely high, medium and low. Thus coefficient of localisation helps in classifying industries according to their dispersion or concentration.

CRITICISM

Though this theory is of considerable use for studying location dynamics of a country and also it helps in deciding the types of industries that may be dispersed under a scheme of regionalism, it has been criticised on the following lines.

1. The theory is not in a position to explain the causes responsible for the choice of location of an industry. It can only help in finding out the existing state of industrial distribution in a country.
2. While finding out coefficient of localisation, the theory makes use of political regions. But it is criticised that the choice should be economic regions but not political regions.
3. The theory says that the localisation for all the countries is the same. But it cannot be the same because distribution of workers in each country varies according to local conditions.
4. The theory considers only workers as the indicator of concentration of an industry, but there is no logic In choosing this one factor alone for finding out concentration of an Industry.
5. The theory has not given due place and consideration to various forces of concentration which have direct bearing on the location of industrial units namely the role of external economies or tax Incentives etc.

7. MONEY MARKET

Money Market plays a key role in any country's economic development. In General market means, a geographical area where traders and buyers run their business transactions. Money market can be said as a place where money can be purchased and sold. In other words, the transactions in money market does not relate to a single good or service. Those transactions relate to money only.

Money market deals with short term trade bills, promissory notes, short term securities issued by the Government. All these papers have high liquidity. In one word we can say that capital market deals with long term loans and money market deals with short term loans. Commercial banks play important role in money market. Because they lend their surplus reserves as short term loans. In the opinion of Reserve Bank of India money market is 'a Centre which deals with short term liquid assets'. It provides short term loans. In the same way it also provides liquidity to the creditors.

FUNCTIONS OF MONEY MARKET

The following are the functions of money market.

1. It provides short term loans to financial end non-financial institutions.
2. It helps the entrepreneurs, industrialists, and traders to meet their temporary needs by providing short term loans.
3. It also provides the necessary short term loans to the Government.
4. It helps as a bridge to the central bank in its money control,

DIVISIONS OF MONEY MARKETS

Money market have the following divisions.

Call money market

This market provides very short term loans. The duration is one day. For stock exchange brokers and dealers it may be less than a week. Commercial banks lend these loans without any security. But these loans are not profitable.

Collateral loan market

In this market, loans are given based on bonds, stocks and securities. The duration of the loans are for few months. The securities are returned immediately after loan repayment.

Bill market

It is also called as discount market. This market deals with short term bills and treasury bills. Generally the duration of the bills is three months. These commercial bills can be discounted. Bills issued by the Government are treated as treasury bills.

Acceptance market

This market deals with the acceptance of banks. The documents issued on banks to pay a certain amount on certain date are called banks' acceptances. As these documents have banks' acceptance, they are circulated in the market.

CHARACTERISTICS OF DEVELOPED MARKET

The highly developed money market has the following features.

1. Central bank plays a key role by having control on various institutions in the market.

2. It has an organised banking system which leads to an organised interest system also. It helps the central bank to have hold on taking decision on interest rates.
3. Because of the organised banking system, commercial banks deal with short term loans and other financial institutions deal with long term loans.
4. Though there are different sectors to deal with different documents they does not compete each other.
5. This market is influenced severely by the financial and political changes in the country.

INDIAN MONEY MARKET

Unlike the organised money market, India's money market is an unorganised one. This market has mainly two parts. One, organised sector, two unorganised sector. Indian Reserve Bank, Commercial banks, co-operative banks, development banks and Post Office savings banks are in organised sector. Indigenous bankers like chettiars, marvadies, middlemen, chitfunds and investment companies are in unorganised sector.

FEATURES OF MONEY MARKET

The following are the features of Indian money market.

1. Demand for money is seasonal in India. It changes according to the agricultural seasons. This is the main feature of Indian money market.
2. The market for Government securities is very less. This is due to inability of Indian reserve bank to implement open market operations.
3. Then would not be much demand for commercial bills and treasury bills.

DEFECTS OF INDIAN MONEY MARKET

Before the inception of Reserve Bank of India, most of the Indian money was unorganised, Indigenous, bankers

Structure of Indian money market

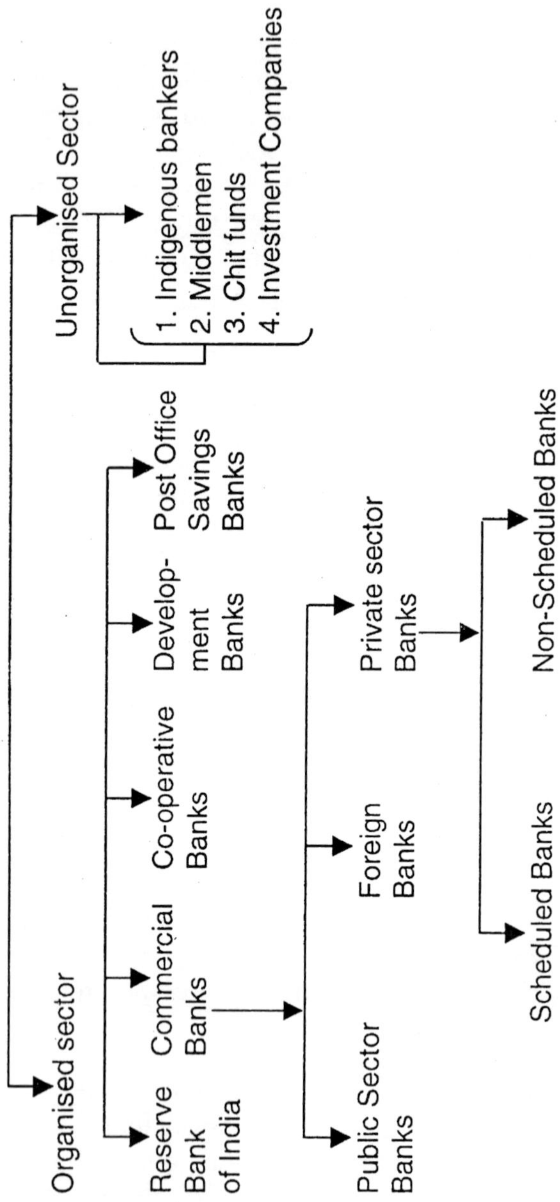

used play prominent role. After the establishment of Reserve Bank of India and nationalisation of commercial banks, the situation changed to some extent. Still there are many defects in Indian money market. They are as follows:

Defect in Co-ordination

Existence of different sectors and absence of proper relation among them are the severe defects of Indian money market. Once, Commercial banks, co-operative banks and indigenous bankers were limited to certain businesses. They would not have any relation with others. They often compete each other. Indian joint stock banks were Jealous of imperial bank and foreign exchange banks. Organised and unorganised systems were completely different. Recently, after Reserve Banks' control over organised sector, the situation has changed for betterment to some extent. Now the organised sector is leading the money market.

Existence of unorganised sector

Existence of indigenous bankers representing unorganised sector is the weakness of Indian money market. They Implement their own decisions in Issuing loans and fixing Interest rates. They are out of the purview of Reserve bank.

Different interest rates

Different Interest rates are used to prevail in the Indian money market. At present though there are no differences in interest rates, the money market is not like a developed money market. Besides, region to region the interest rates are different. This is because of slow distribution of funds from one region to the other.

Seasonal demand for money

Another weakness of Indian money market is demand for short term funds is seasonal. Either increase or decrease of demand for money depends on agricultural crops.

Unexpanded bill market

Reserve bank of India is unable to control inflation and loans of commercial banks through open market operations due to less market to Government securities in the money market. The 'Bill Market Scheme' of 1952 introduced by Reserve Bank failed to provide bill market in India. In fact, this scheme provided an opportunity to commercial banks to take loans from Reserve Bank. Anyhow, Reserve bank introduced new bill market scheme in 1970 to deal with short term bills. In spite of Reserve banks' work, the bill market scheme is not successful.

Banking system

Indian banking system is not fully developed. Until very recently branch expansion does not reach momentum. This is also one of the reasons for weak money market in India.

Unable to attract foreign funds

Because of undeveloped bill market and having unorganised departments influence, it is unable to attract foreign funds. Though the condition in recent years changed to some extent, but it is not to the expected level.

CONCLUSION

From the above discussion it is clear, that the money market in India has to be developed a lot. Though the money market is developed in recent years, bill market and acceptance market which have to play key role in money market are not completely formed. Treasury bills and trade bills which are the main source of short term funds are not coming much in practice. Indian money market is unable to attract funds from other money markets and from foreign investors. However, we can say that the Indian money market made some progress in performing the functions and developing the relation between groups.

8. CAPITAL MARKET

Capital market is a market which provides capital to industrial and business houses on long term basis. It depends on personal savings and Government money. Some times the term is used in a very broad sense to include also the market for short term funds.

DEFINITION

Ex: Living stone defines capital market as follows:

"It is the business of the capital market to facilitate the movement of the steam of command over capital, to the point of highest yield".

NATURE AND CONSTITUENTS

The capital market consists number of individuals and institutions that channelise the supply of and demand for long term capital and claims on capital. The stock exchanges, commercial banks, co-operative banks, savings banks, development banks. Insurance companies. Investment trusts or companies etc., are the Important constituents of the capital market.

The capital market, like money market, has three important components, namely, the suppliers of loanable funds, the borrowers and the Intermediaries who deal with the lenders on the one hand and the borrowers on the other.

In the capital market, the supply of funds comes from individual and corporate savings, institutional investors and the surplus of Governments. The demand for capital comes from agriculture, trade, industry and the Government.

With the emergence of joint stock companies as the predominant form of industrial organisation, developed capital market become a necessary infrastructure for rapid Industrialisation. Business firms can raise funds from the capital market by issuing shares and credit instruments. The capital market is not concerned solely with the issue of new claims on capital, but also with dealings in existing claims. In fact, the marketability of securities is an important element in the efficient working of the capital market, for investors would be reluctant to make loans if their claims are not be easily disposed off.

The developed countries have comparatively well-developed money and capital markets. But In developing countries, the capital market, like the money market is generally under developed.

CAPITAL MARKET IN INDIA

The Indian capital market consists of an organised sector and an unorganised sector. In the organised market, the demand for capital comes from mostly from corporate enterprises, Government and semi-Government institutions and the supply comes from house hold savings. Institutional Investors like banks, Investment trusts, insurance companies, finance corporations, Government and international financing agencies.

The unorganised market consists mostly of indigenous bankers and money lenders on the supply side. While in the organised sector, the demand for funds is mostly for productive investment, a large part of the demand for funds in the unorganised market is for consumption purposes. In fact, many purposes for which funds are very difficult to get from the organised are financed by the unorganised sector. Like the unorganised money market, the unorganised capital market in India is characterised by the existence of a multiplicity of interest rates, exorbitant rates of interest and lack of uniformity in their business dealings.

While the activities of the organised market are subject to a number of Government controls, the unorganised sector is, by and large, out side effective Government control.

The organised sector has been subjected to increasing institutionalisation. A large part of the business of this sector is accounted for by the public sector financial institutions, and the Government control over other segments of the organised capital market has increased over the years.

DEVELOPMENT OF THE MARKET

The important factors that contributed to the development of Indian capital market are as follows:

Legislation measures

Laws like Companies Act, the securities contracts (Regulation) Act and the capital issues (control) Act empowered the Government to regulate the activities of the capital market with a view to ensuring healthy trends in the market, protecting the interests of investors, and ensuring an efficient utilisation of the resources etc.

Expansion of development banks and public sector

Starting with the establishment of the IFCI, a number of development banks have been established at the national and regional levels to provide financial and other development assistance to entrepreneurs and enterprises.

The expansion of the public sector in the money market and capital markets has been accelerated by nationalisation of the Insurance business and a major part of the banking business.

Growth of under writing business

There has been a phenomenal growth in the under writing business. After the elimination of forward trading, brokers have begun to take underwriting risks in the new issues market.

Public Confidence

The impressive performance of certain large companies encouraged public investment in industrial securities.

Awareness

The improvements in education and communication have created increasing public awareness of the Investment opportunity in the business sector.

DEFECTS OF CAPITAL MARKET

The capital market in India has not developed to the desired extent due to the following defects.

High tax rates

Taxation rates in India have been increasing very fast. Most of the savings of the people go away by way of taxes. This has resulted in the starvation of capital market.

Lack of awareness

Public on the whole is not quite aware of the importance of well developed and properly organised capital market. Because of this reason, the savings of the public are not fully available to capital market.

Lack of advisory bodies

Lack of investment advisory bodies is also one of the reasons for defective capital market in India. Because in India most of the people are rural based and illiterate. They must be educated regarding the methods, importance and profits of savings. Then only the required money may flow to the capital market.

Influence of unorganised capital markets

Unorganised capital, market depends on local brokers and businessmen doing interest business. The transactions in this market may not go with rules and regulations.

Organised capital market may not develop, due to this type of unorganised capital market.

STEPS TAKEN FOR REMOVING DEFECTS OF CAPITAL MARKET

The following are the steps taken for removing defects of capital market in India.

1. To protect the deposits of public, Government made Companies Act 1956, capital issues Act, MRTP Act etc.
2. During recent years underwriting activities of many financial institutions have made satisfactory progress. This has given sufficient encouragement to business activity in the country.
3. Commercial banks have encouraged growth of capital market by granting more advances against shares and debentures. These banks also make their funds available to finance corporations by purchasing their shares and debentures.
4. Many sound financial institutions have been set up to provide short and long term advances for industrial advancement and growth of the country.
5. The formation of Industrial development bank of India and unit trust of India have also contributed a lot in the capital market and in its proper organisation.
6. The growth of joint stock form of business, the expanding role of Reserve bank, the establishment of various corporations and the Government assistance to Industry have contributing for the development of capital market in India.

9. STOCK EXCHANGES

We know regularised markets for purchase and sale of goods. In the same, manner, there are special markets for purchase and sale of securities. A regularised market for purchase and sale of industrial, financial and Government securities is called as 'stock exchange'. In this market, purchase and sale of already issued shares and included in authorised list of stock exchange transactions take place. The securities include, equity shares, preference shares and debentures of companies Government bonds, and bonds and debentures issued by local bodies.

MEANING

As per the securities contracts (Regulation) Act, 1956 stock exchange means—

"A registered or unregistered society, organisation or group of persons with the objective of helping the sale and purchase transactions of securities, their regularisation and control is called stock exchange".

IMPORTANCE

Stock exchanges are in key place in every country's capital market and economy, stock exchanges are helping for large scale propagating of joint stock company organisation. Stock exchanges are also helping the people who have invested in company securities, to get back their money as and when they like. People come forward to invest their savings in company securities because, stock exchanges are providing uninterrupted sale and purchase of securities. Stock exchanges also frame rules and regulations to check cheating transactions.

Securities get organised and continuous market through stock exchanges. As the transactions and the members are with in the purview of rules and regulations, there is possibility for impartial transactions of securities. Stock exchanges have experienced members who follow rules and regulations strictly. This helps in change of prices of securities according to the management, profit earning and financial position of the issued organisations. Hence investors can sell their securities to their real values. Because stock exchanges are doing business of securities relating to business and commercial organisations, they are usually called 'business of businesses'.

FUNCTIONS OF STOCK EXCHANGES

The following are the financial functions of stock exchanges.

Ready and continuous market

Stock exchanges keep ready and continuous market for purchase, sale and transfer of various securities freely and easily.

Provision of liquidity to securities

Stock exchanges help to change securities easily into cash. Investors, at the time of requirement can get cash by selling their securities.

Fixing of prices of securities

The prices of securities which reflect the market value are fixed in stock exchanges. Generally, the prices of securities depend on their demand and supply. Stock exchanges record the prices at which the purchasers and sellers of securities settled the rates.

Protection to investors

By implementing strict rules, stock exchanges give protection to the investors without giving any trouble to their interest. If there were no stock exchanges, the innocent investors may be cheated by the clever and experienced brokers.

Regularisation of companies management

Those securities which are included in the authorised list of a stock exchange are only allowed for sale and purchase in that stock exchange. Companies which want to include their shares and debentures in the list of stock exchange, have to obey the rules of that stock exchange. In this way stock exchanges indirectly regularising the companies management.

Helping for additional capital

If companies (having good financial structure) securities, are sold for higher prices for a long time, public wants to buy such securities. Because of this, profitable companies can mobilise the necessary additional capital easily.

Helping for country's capital formation

People are being attracted towards investment in securities because of the facilities for ready and regular market, advertisement, display of prices of Government and commercial securities by the stock exchanges. This helps the Government and industries in formulating the required sources.

Helping for speculative

Stock exchanges provide facilities to the skilled businessmen to earn profits through speculation. Modern communication system provides the prices of securities immediately. Speculators by using this facility, by securities at low prices in one exchange and sell them at high prices in the other.

SERVICES OF STOCK EXCHANGES

Stock exchanges are providing valuable services to the companies, investors and society. They are discussed here under.

Services to Companies

Deposit mobilisation is easy for companies through stock exchanges. Companies follows high standards for registration at stock exchanges. This helps them in getting loans from banks and financial institutions. Stock exchange is also useful to ascertain the value of securities at the time of amalgamation and absorption, companies, through big market get wide publicity.

Services to investors

Exchanges are providing many services to investors. They provide liquidity to securities and security intransactions. Investors can get loans by keeping the securities as collateral security. They can know the prices of securities whenever they require. As stock exchanges are providing information on securities through statistics and statements, investors can select the profitable securities easily. There would not be any risk in buying securities at stock exchanges.

Service to society

With the facilities provided by stock exchanges, the corporate system will develop and this leads to industrial progress. Stock exchanges by providing liquidity to securities, are encouraging the people for investment. It helps in capital formation of the country. Sufficient capital helps in increasing companies management standards.

Stock exchanges help in mobilising the required sources to the Government for development activities which have national importance. Stock exchanges are also useful in converting public sayings into productive purposes and thus help in achieving economic development.

10. SECURITIES CONTRACTS (REGULATION) ACT, 1956

To run the stock exchanges uninterruptedly and in reasonable manner, pure and lawful speculation to the required volume is a must. But, if the speculation becomes gambling, the expected advantages from the stock exchanges will become impossible. The speculators may adopt undesirable methods in securities transactions. Hence, an agency is required to show the difference between healthy and pure speculation and unhealthy gambling.

In the year 1921, Government thought of regularising undesirable speculative transactions in Indian Stock exchanges. In 1925, to regulate Bombay stock exchange. Bombay securities contracts (Regulation) Act was made. In 1944, to review the working of stock exchanges, an enquiry was made by money research division. After the reports of Thomas Committee (1948), Gorvola committee (1951) and the recommendations of chambers of commerce, stock exchanges, at last in 1954 'Securities Contracts (Regulation) bill' was submitted to parliament for acceptance. After parliament's acceptance in 1956 it became act.

DEFECTS IN STOCK EXCHANGES (BEFORE THE ACT)

The following were the defects of stock exchanges before 'Securities Contracts (Regulation) Act, 1956 was made.

1. Because of absence of a central organisation, the system of working and rules of various stock exchanges are used to be different.
2. Absence of rules regarding membership gave an opportunity to many undesirable persons to get membership and earn secret profits.
3. Absence of Government's control over stock exchanges made many people to take up speculative businesses. In experienced people used to become insolvents.
4. Absence of limit on the number of stock exchanges at a place made to establish more than one stock exchange

at cities like Bombay and Calcutta. This atmosphere resulted in more speculative transactions in stock exchanges.

5. Absence of rules to include the securities in stock exchange list made all companies (whether their capital structure is strong or weak) to include their securities in the list. This resulted in increase of speculative business and the prices of securities fixed were also unreal.

To rectify the above defects the securities contracts Act was made.

SECURITIES CONTRACTS (REGULATION) ACT - CONDITIONS

The following are the main conditions of the act.

Recognition of stock exchanges

The act permits only recognised stock exchanges to do securities transactions. In each city more than one stock exchange can not work. The unrecognised exchanges will be treated as unlawful. The exchanges, which want recognition should follow certain conditions.

Central Government's Control over stock exchanges

Government has many powers to control stock exchanges. It has power to ask the required information, to enquire on their transactions and members, to cancel their working committees, to close the business for seven days in emergency, to stop undesired speculation and to order for auditing books.

Regulation of management

Securities contracts Act gave power to the Government to regulate managerial transactions through rules of stock exchanges. The Government has powers to include securities in the list of stock exchange, to fix the rates of brokerage and commission, to fix market rates in emergency conditions, to settle quarrels and claims etc.

Restrictions on Speculation

As per the act, the vacantly transfer period should not exceed more than two months. It declared all option transactions after the act came into existence are illegal. All Kerb transactions which took place outside the stock exchange are prohibited.

DIRECTORATE OF STOCK EXCHANGES

To regulate stock exchanges and to implement the rules In Securities Contracts Act, 1956, Indian Government has established a Directorate of stock exchanges in the year 1959. It has its head office at Bombay and branches at Calcutta and Delhi.

The directorate observes the working of stock exchanges and business activities of members. It suggests stock exchanges in restricting unhealthy speculative transactions. It works to stop illegal option and Kerb transactions. It issues licenses to persons to do securities business. It also acts impartially towards companies. In this way the directorate acts as a co-ordinator between Government and stock exchanges.

SECURITIES CONTRACTS (REGULATION) ACT, 1956 - CRITICISM

Though the Securities Contracts (Regulation) Act was brought into regulate speculative business and to restrict unfair transactions is subject to the following criticisms.

1. Some criticise the act on the ground that it restricts the internal freedom of stock exchanges.
2. Some others criticise the act on the ground that it does not have proper conditions to control undesired speculative corners and wash sales.

3. As the act has not prohibited adjourn business which helps for speculation, it is criticised that this opportunity may make the speculators reckless and irresponsible.

11. INDUSTRIAL POLICIES

Industrial development is a must for economic development of a country. If we can see the economic progress of developed countries it is understood that the reason behind their success is industrial development. Hence to define the role of private, public and other sectors, an industrial policy should be there.

The British Government failed to introduce any industrial policy in our country. It's policies instead, spoiled the industrialisation. In the year 1944, before we get independence. Planning and development department has been established. On April 21, 1945 by issuing an industrial policy note, it defines the role of public and private sectors.

INDUSTRIAL POLICY RESOLUTION 1948

After attaining independence, on 6th April 1948, the Government Introduced the first industrial policy. It explains the need for industrial productivity, proper distribution and Governments' role in achieving them. The following were the main aspects of the policy.

Role of Public and Private Sector

The policy defined Public and Private sectors as per the economic system (mixed economy) of our country. It divided industries and made clear regarding their productive activities. The Public Sector has been given much preference than Private Sector.

Classification of Industries

The large Industries have been divided into four categories:

a) Industries with absolute monopoly of the States

Manufactures of arms and ammunitions, production and control of atomic energy and ownership and management of railway transport were included in this category. These industries are to be under the absolute monopoly of the state.

b) Basic industries

Government only starts the basic industries like coal, iron, steal, manufacturing of aeroplanes and ships etc., some of these industries already in the hands private organisations shall be taken over by the Government slowly.

c) Industries to continue under the Government control

Industries in this category were subjected to the control and regulation of the Central Government in consultation with the provincial Government concerned. It comprised of 18 basic industries such as automobiles, heavy chemicals, heavy machinery, fertilisers electricals etc.

d) Industries under Private Sector

The rest of the industries not covered by the above three categories were included in this category. It was opened to private enterprise, individuals and co-operatives. However, the state was allowed to enter even into this field.

Role of village and small scale industries

The policy resolution identified the need of village and small industries for economic development. It wanted to concentrate on the problems of these industries.

Foreign Capital

The policy resolution wanted the Government to impose certain restrictions on the quantum of foreign capital flow into the country. Such restrictions were conceived necessary to avoid impact of foreign capital on the Indian economic scene in future.

INDUSTRIAL POLICY RESOLUTION 1956

There were many changes in the country due to first industrial policy. In the same period the First Five Year Plan was also completed. In this Juncture, the Government declared new industrial policy resolution in the year 1956, The following were the various factors included in the policy.

Division of industries

The industrial policy made it clear that the key and basic industries should be in public sector for planned development in the society. This results in division of industries into three categories.

a) Industries under state monopoly

Arms, iron, steel, coal, electricity etc., 18 industries were kept under schedule 'A'. Government will look after the development of these industries.

b) Industries to come under state ownership

Aluminium, fertilisers, machine tools etc., 12 industries were included in Schedule 'B'. These industries may slowly be taken over by the Government.

c) Industries under private sector

Rest of the industries were left to private sector. Government also help these industries to prosper.

Cottage, Village and Small Scale Industries

The industrial policy wanted to give some concessions to cottage, village and small scale industries, as they are necessary for country's development. Hence, the policy decided to increase the competitive capacity of these industries.

Rectification of regional disparities

To rectify the regional disparities in the country, the industrial policy resolution decided to take up Industrialisation in backward areas.

Development of technical and managerial personnel

Technical and managerial personnel are necessary for industrial development. Hence, the policy resolution stressed the need to improve the training facilities in universities and other institutions.

Industrial peace

Industrial peace is one of the essential conditions for industrial development. To achieve this, the policy resolved to have workers participation in management. It also suggested to improve the efficiency of the workers by providing them sufficient facilities.

Management of public enterprises

The industrial policy identified the need for the commercial development of public enterprises. The policy says, that it is the duty of the Government to provide funds for their development.

Foreign capital

The policy decided to reduce foreign investment in industries to 40 percent.

The Industrial Policy resolution of 1956 was wider in scope when compared to the resolution of 1948. It discussed very clearly the role of public and private sector and the co-operation between them for industrialisation.

INDUSTRIAL POLICY RESOLUTIONS, 1973, 1977

The industrial policy Resolution, 1956 was continued uninterruptedly up to 1973. Basing on the recommendations of planning commission and administrative reforms committee, slight changes were made in the policy in 1973. The Government accepted to form 'Joint Sector' on the recommendations of Dutt Committee. The policy of 1973 declared many concessions to both Indian and foreign institutions.

The Janata Government after came into power, declared a new industrial policy on 23rd December, 1977. This resolution gave much importance to small and household industries. It recommended many measures to regulate the activities of big institutions. It also discussed the aspects like location of industries, industrial sickness etc. But it can be said that this resolution had not bring much change in the basic structure of the industrial policy, 1956.

INDUSTRIAL POLICY RESOLUTION 1980

After recapturing of power by the Congress Government at centre. It proposed a new industrial policy resolution on July 23, 1980 basing on 1956 resolution. The following were the various factors included in the industrial policy, 1980.

Economic and Social Objects

This resolution made it clear the economic and the social objectives. It aims at complete utilisation of productive capacity, improving the productivity, encouraging the exports, creating employment opportunities, regional balance and consumers protection etc.

Steps to improve the performance of public enterprises

The industrial policy resolved to improve the working of public enterprises. It also suggested to analyse the working and take necessary steps of each organisation to improve their managerial performance.

Village and Small Scale Industries

The policy increased the investment limits of these industries. In view of increased costs, it recognised the need for increasing the limits. A small scale unit investment limit in plant and machinery increased to Rs. 20 lakhs.

Private Sector

Private industries can widen their activities, if such activities would not lead to monopoly.

Storage of key raw materials

To face the raw material problem of small scale industries, the Industrial policy felt the need for storage of key raw materials. For the time being the co-operation and co-ordination of small scale industries corporation (SSIC) was sought.

Development of backward areas

To reduce the imbalances the policy suggested to declare some concessions to backward areas development.

Increase in productive capacity

The policy thought of increasing the productive capacity in various big industries. It provided facility to increase the productive capacity to 25 per cent, at 5 per cent increase for 5 years.

Industrial sickness

The policy asked the Government to introduce proper control method to check wide spread industrial sickness in industries. The policy also expected measures like concessions in income and take over of sick units by healthy units.

Technical know-how

Government, after recognising the lapse of competitive capacity in foreign markets, gave preference to technical knowledge. It gives incentives for quick transfer of technical knowledge from efficient organisations to new organisations. It also takes steps for improvement in research and development sectors.

Modernisation

Government brought to light the need for modernisation of out dated industries through this policy resolution. It also applicable to small scale industries.

Environmental pollution

The industrial policy resolution expressed its fear on environmental pollution. It asked the industries to take steps to avoid pollution. Government thought of attaining this objective through decentralisation of industries.

Some people criticised the policy on the ground that it is meaningless, unclear and political. But some others felt that it clearly expressed the policies of the Government.

INDUSTRIAL POLICY RESOLUTION, 1990

The industrial policy resolution proposed by Janata Dal Government, suggested delicencing policy.

It also suggested to increase the maximum limit of investment on small scale industries to Rs. 60 lakhs and on tiny units to Rs. 5 lakhs.

It resolved to encourage foreign investments in industries.

This resolution was also criticised as political and meaningless.

INDUSTRIAL POLICY RESOLUTION, 1991

After recapturing of power by the Congress Government in mid-term polls, declared its new industrial policy resolution. It is understood, that the policy is made keeping in view the industrial policy resolution of 1990. The following are some of the Important factors in the policy.

Delicencing

License hurdles have been removed to encourage industrialists to start more industries. Except for the notified 18 types of industries, the other industries need no license. Now the industrialists or the entrepreneurs need not take the risk of filling number of forms and waiting for permission.

Foreign investment

To attract foreign investments in India, the industrial policy resolution increased the foreign investments limit from 40 per cent to 51 per cent. Before this resolution, no foreign investor have given an opportunity to hold majority (51 per cent or above) shares in Indian companies.

Encouragement to exports

To face foreign exchange problem, the policy resolved to give more support to exports.

More help to small-scale sector

This industrial policy gave much importance to labour oriented and capital sparing small scale sector. It increased the investment limit in plant and machinery to Rs. 60 lakhs for small scale industries, to Rs. 75 lakhs for ancillary industries and to Rs. 5 lakhs for tiny units. It also resolved to continue the reservation policy, subsidies and incentives to encourage small sector. Later, the investment limit in small scale industries increased to Rs. 1 crore.

12. INDUSTRIAL LICENSING POLICY

When we contemplate planned economic development, it is obvious that the Government must have the instrument of industrial licensing to regulate effectively all industrial activities in a mixed economy. A license is an official written permission to start and run an industry. It describes all essential details such as location, articles to be produced, the capacity of the industrial unit, period to achieve the maximum permitted utilisation of capacity etc.

OBJECTIVES

Industrial licensing is an instrument to implement the industrial policy objectives. These objectives are derived from the main goals of our development plans namely, growth, self-reliance, social and distributive justice. The following are the objectives of industrial licensing policy:

1. to develop and regulate industrial investment and productivity according to the importance and objectives of development plans,
2. to give protection and encouragement to small and medium scale industries,
3. to control concentration of economic power, and
4. to obtain regional equilibrium among various regions.

INDUSTRIES ACT, 1951

To achieve the above mentioned objectives. Industries (Development and Regulation) Act was made in the year 1951. The main objective of the act is to develop and regulate the private industrial sector according to the planning policy and other social and political policies.

Objectives

The other objectives of the act are as follows:

1. Optimum utilisation of the country's available resources.
2. Balanced development of large scale and small scale industries.
3. Diversification of various industries.
4. Regulation of production, distribution, prices and other such matters, and if necessary, to take over the management of enterprises under certain conditions.

5. Establishment of Development Councils for industrial planning.

Under this legislation, Government got powers to issue licenses for starting new industries, expansion of existing enterprise, manufacture of new article etc., as per the Industrial Policy resolution of 1948.

A license is necessary for starting new business enterprise, manufacturing a new product by present unit, expanding the industrial capacity substantially, changing location of present business and carrying on the business of existing unit which did not have a license so far.

LETTER OF INTENT

With in a month of deposit of an application for an Industrial license, a letter of intent is issued. The industry concerned is called upon to submit terms of foreign collaboration, import of machinery and equipment, terms of issue of capital and such other relevant details within one year. Six months' extension is possible only twice for clearance of information. As soon as conditions mentioned in the letter of intent are honoured, an industrial license is issued in due course.

CRITERIA FOR GRANT OF LICENSE

The Criteria for grant of a license are :

i) Industrial policy and industrial licensing policy
ii) Priorities under Five Year Plans
iii) tochno-economic conditions of a particular industry
iv) techno-economic features indicating the viability of the proposed project, its foreign exchange needs, location, new materials supply etc.
v) export objectives, international demand, import substitution prospects, and
vi) use of domestic know-how.

INDUSTRIAL LICENSING POLICY, 1970, 1973

Industrial policy resolution of 1956, provides the frame work for the regulation of industries. The statement of February 1970 and that of February 1973 are the two policy statements mostly modifying the industrial licensing system on the basis of recommendations made by the Administrative Reforms Commission (1967) and the Industrial Licensing Policy Inquiry Committee (1969). Under February 1970 amendments 5 groups of industries were introduced. They are

i) Core Sector,
ii) heavy investment sector
iii) 'middle sector'
iv) joint sector, and
v) small scale sector.

In February 1973, the policy was revised further by rationalising the list of industries and improving the definitions of the aforesaid sectors. The following are the features of the Industrial Policy 1973.

Revised licensing procedures will ensure

1. expansion of the public sector.
2. establishment of reserved industries in the small industries sector.
3. Preference for small and medium entrepreneurs relation to larger home or foreign companies.
4. Implementation of restrictions on larger companies.
5. Regulation of foreign concerns.
6. Working of Joint sector.

Public Sector expansion

17 basic; strategic industries and public utility and other essential industries involving large capital investment will be in the public sector. Thus, the so-called core sector is reserved exclusively for state enterprise.

Small sector

Small sector include those units with fixed capital up to Rs. 10 lakhs and in the case of ancillary industry up to Rs. 15 lakhs. The manufacture of certain articles, as specified will be reserved only for the small sector.

Preference to small and medium concerns

Co-operatives, small and medium units will be encouraged in the production of mass consumption goods along with the public sector.

Larger industrial houses

These are the undertakings having an asset value of at-least Rs. 20 crore. These larger industrial houses will be eligible along with others to participate only in certain industries specified on the policy statement of February 1973 provided the items are not reserved for the public and small sectors. The list covers 19 groups.

Regulation of foreign investment

Foreign investment will be subject to the guidelines on the dilution of foreign equity and foreign Exchange Regulation Act, 1973.

Joint Sector

The Joint sector concept was an innovation introduced by the new industrial licensing policy. It involves partnership between

a) Governments
b) Government Corporations and
c) Private Entrepreneurs.

INDUSTRIAL LICENSING POLICY 1975

In 1975, Government declared new industrial licensing policy to regulate industrial licensing system. It cancelled licensing policy with regard to 21 industries. It permitted the expansion of productive capacity in case of 30 main industries. But this permission is granted only when the additional production is exported or sold as per the Government norms.

INDUSTRIAL LICENSING POLICY, 1978

To look into the licensing system. Government appointed an enquiry committee in 1977 under the chairmanship of Sri G.P. Rama Krishna. The Government accepted all the recommendations made by the committee. As per the 1978 licensing policy, the investment limit required to get license. Increased from Rs. I crore to Rs. 3 crore and thus the licensing system liberalised. But the foreign exchange required to import raw materials and tools should not exceed Rs. 25 lakhs or 10 per cent of annual production whichever is less. And at the same time the goods produced by these industries should not belong to the allotted items of public sector or small scale sector. It does not apply to the dominating companies and companies having foreign capital more than 40 per cent.

Industrial Licensing Policy, 1980

The new Industrial licensing policy was declared in July, 1980. The many aspects of the policy are as follows:

1. Increase in productive capacity due to technical development and increase in labour productivity is natural. This type of increase is allowed up to 25 per cent at 5 per cent per year for the first 5 years.
2. For the development of small scale industries, the investment limit increased from Rs. 10 lakhs to Rs. 20 lakhs and in case of ancillary units the limit increased from Rs. 15 lakhs to Rs. 25 lakhs. This facilitates modernisation in small scale sector. Again in 1985, the investment limit increased to Rs. 35 lakhs for small units and to Rs. 45 lakhs for ancillary units.

INDUSTRIAL LICENSING POLICY 1990, 1991

In 1990, Janata Dal Government introduced a new industrial licensing policy. According to this policy, no license is required for starting a new industry. But before the policy get its complete shape, the Government has changed and again a new licensing policy is declared by the Congress Government in 1991.

The main features of the industrial licensing policy, 1991 are as follows:

1. No license is required to start an industrial unit. But, this does not apply to 18 main industries listed by the Government.
2. The limit of foreign investments in Indian industries increased from 40 per cent to 51 per cent.
3. The investment limit in small scale units, ancillary units and tiny units increased to Rs. 60 lakhs, Rs. 75 lakhs and Rs. 5 lakhs respectively.
4. Incentives will be given to those units which produce the export oriented goods.

From the above discussion, we can say that the industrial licensing policy in India after various turns ended with delicensing policy.

13. CONCENTRATION OF ECONOMIC POWER

Though the directive principles of the state policy have clearly envisaged that India will be a socialistic state, yet dispersal of wealth did not take place. Dr. R.K. Hazari pointed out that by 1958, 20 leading monopolies had invested Rs. 352 crore in 1073 companies. Before nationalisation of banks, these were controlled by few industrial houses who controlled 70 per cent of the news papers agencies and business, These business houses also controlled production and distribution of 75 per cent of the total consumption goods and 65 per cent daily consumption goods. In this way it is clear that industries got concentrated only in few hands and few business houses began to a mass wealth.

CONCENTRATION ECONOMIC POWER - REASONS

Some of the important reasons responsible for concentration of economic power are briefly discussed as under:

Failure of financial institutions

In India many financial institutions were set up with huge authorised capital. The main idea of setting up these institutions was that those houses which were financially weak should be assisted. But Instead of this, the financial assistance was provided to financially sound and large industrial houses resulting in concentration of economic power or wealth only in few industrial houses.

Licensing policy of the Government

This is also one among the reasons for concentration of economic power. Government, by keeping industrial development in view, followed liberal licensing policy before 1969. Big industrial houses acquired many licenses, by exploiting this opportunity.

Help from commercial banks

Before nationalisation commercial banks used to help big industrialists. This resulted in development of only few industries.

Defective legal system

After independence, the Government was very keen that the country should speedily and quickly grow in the industrial field. For this purpose, certain laws were passed and tax concessions were also given. But there were many lacunas in these laws and big industrial houses took full advantage of these defects.

No check on industrial houses

No efforts were made to check the influence of big industrial houses with the result that these continued to get benefits from all sources.

MEASURES TO CHECK CONCENTRATION OF ECONOMIC POWER

The following are some of the measures suggested to check concentration of economic power

1. It is suggested that while issuing licenses new entrepreneurs should be encouraged and big industrial houses should be issued licenses for large sectors only.
2. Commercial banks should be instructed to extend financial assistance to small rather than large scale industries.
3. Legislative measures should be taken on industrial houses which violate law and indulge in malpractices.
4. Government should encourage different types of small scale units for equal development of all regions.
5. It is also necessary to increase public enterprises.
6. Special incentives should be given to new entrepreneurs (excluding big industrialists) coming forward to start industries in backward areas.

GOVERNMENT COMMITTEES

To avoid concentration of economic power in few hands, Government has appointed many committees and commissions to enquire on this matter. Besides, it also made some enactments. After these measures it can be said that the situation in our country changed to better after the year 1970. Let us discuss on these committees and acts.

Mahalanobis Committee (1960)

Mahalanobis Committee was set up under the Chairmanship of Sri P.C. Mahalanobis in October 1960. Terms of references of the committee were to find out how far additional income generated in the first and second plan had been spread in the country and also to review the changes in the levels of living during plan periods. Then the Committee was also required to find out trends in the distribution of income and wealth and to Identify gaps in statistical data which were essential for a penetrating study of the type.

Suggestions

The Committee felt that the wealth had been got excessive concentrated in few hands and that in the process big financial institutions had contributed by loaning heavy amounts to few industrial houses. It felt that it was desirable to further study how far such a concentration was inevitable. It recommended that the role of private sector in the national economy should not be under estimated and a full time agency appointed to study the matter.

Monopolies Enquiry Commission (1964)

Monopolies enquiry Commission was set up in April, 1964 with Sri K.C. Das Gupta, a judge of Supreme Court as its Chairman. The Commission submitted its report in October, 1965.

The Commission was required to enquire into the nature and effects of concentration of economic power into private hands.

The Commission pointed out various causes responsible for the concentration of economic power. These included development of joint stock companies, money a massed during second world war and unhealthy and defective system of issuing licenses. It pointed out industries in which there was concentration and those in which there was no concentration. In view of the commission, concentration had resulted in many evil consequences including corruption in business. It recommended to set up a permanent body to avoid concentration of wealth in few hands. It also suggested that political parties should not accept donations from big industrial houses.

14. MONOPOLIES AND RESTRICTIVE TRADE PRACTICES ACT (MRTP ACT) 1969

The Monopolies and Restrictive Trade Practices Act was passed by the Parliament in December, 1969 and brought into force with effect from June 1, 1970. Its main objectives are as follows:

OBJECTIVES

1. to control and regulate the concentration of economic power in a few hands of business and industry.
2. to control monopolies and monopolistic trade practices and
3. to prohibit restrictive trade practices unless any one of them can be Justified in the place of interest.

The Government has recently undertaken a set of measures to rationalise the MRTP Act. The asset threshold bringing a unit under the purview of the MRTP Act, which was set at Rs. 20 crore in 1969 was raised to Rs. 100 crore. In March 1985, the Government issued a notification exempting MRTP companies in 27 industries from section 21 and 22 of the Act. In effect, this permitted MRTP companies to directly seek a license under the (D&R) Act without first obtaining prior and separate clearance from the department of company affairs for a new project or substantial expansion.

At the end of December 1985, the Government notified a revised and expanded list of Appendix I industries and new list specifies 30 broad categories of industries in which MRTP companies are permitted to set up capacities, provided the concerned items of manufacture are not specifically reserved for the small scale or public sectors. Out aide the Appendix I industries, MRTP companies will continue to be permitted if the product is predominantly for export. This requires an export share of 60 per cent if the items reserved for the small scale sector.

To promote the role of MRTP companies in the industrialisation of backward areas, the conditions permitting these companies to establish non-Appendix I industries in backward districts have been liberalised. Hither to MRTP companies setting up non-Appendix I industries were required to fulfil an export obligation of 50 per cent in backward districts of categories B and C and 30 per cent in category A. The export obligations have now been reduced to 25 per cent for categories B and C and Zero for category A.

All these measures have reduced barriers to entry into high priority industrial sectors and thus buttressed the competitive forces operating to reduce costs and improve quality.

In recent years, the MRTP Act has already been diverted of several of its stringent restrictive provisions in recent years. Some more proposals like the dilution of the concept of interconnection for defining a company under the Act, are under Government's consideration.

RECENT DEVELOPMENT

Very recently i.e. in September 1991 Government announced that the industries are almost excluded from the purview of MRTP Act. If this proposal is approved and implemented, the MRTP Act would cease to be relevance for the big industrial houses in that the majority of them would be outside the purview of this legislation.

MRTP COMMISSION

The MRTP Commission was set up in August 1970 under the MRTP Act. It is the major wing of the enforcement machinery for the regulation of monopolies and restrictive trade practices in the country. Besides performing certain functions in respect of the prevention of concentration of economic power and control of monopolies, the MRTP commission has to regulate monopolistic and restrictive trade practices. It has a dual character. In matters relating to the prevention of concentration of economic power control of monopolies and monopolistic trade practices, it has to report its opinions or findings to the Government. In respect of restrictive trade practices, it can pass final orders.

Its advisory functions relating to the prevention of concentration of economic power and control of monopolies can be activated only on a reference from the Government. It has to inquire and report its opinion to the Government in the matters of substantial expansion undertakings, the establishment of new undertakings, mergers, amalgamations and takeovers and the division of undertakings.

MRTP Commission can also act on the basis of its own knowledge or information and institute an inquiry, and has to report its findings arrived at after such an inquiry to the Government. The final orders are to be passed by the Government.

NEW COMPETITION POLICY

Recently (2000), the New Competition Policy has been submitted to the Government, formulated by SVS Raghavan Committee. The proposed New Competition Policy, proposes to repeal Monopolies & Restrictive Trade Practices Act, 1969 (MRTP). It states that the essence and spirit of competition should be served while positioning the competition policy and to harmonise the conflict between the Competition Policy and Government policy. The economic reforms of liberalisation, deregulation and privatisation need to be progressed and should be designed in a way that it strengthens the competition policy and vice versa.

SALIENT FEATURES OF NEW COMPETITION POLICY

1. ***The Industries (Development and Regulation) Act, 1951*** may no longer be necessary except for location (avoidance of urban-centric location), for environmental protection and for monuments and national heritage protection considerations, etc.
2. ***The Industrial Disputes Act, 1947*** and the connected statutes need to be amended to provide for an easy exit to the non-viable, ill-managed and inefficient units subject to their legal obligations in respect of their liabilities.
3. The Board for Industrial Finance & Restructure (BIFR) formulated under the provisions of ***Sick industrial Companies (Special Provisions) Act 1985*** should be abolished.
4. ***Trade Practices***
   a) All trade policies should be open, non-discriminatory and rule bound.
   b) Anti-Competitive practices should be considered as illegal. Blatant price, quantity, bid and territory sharing agreements and cartels should be considered as illegal.

5. State Monopolies: The State monopolies and public enterprises should fall under the Competition Policy to prevent monopolistic, restrictive and unfair trade practices. The State Government should divest its shares and assets in State monopolies and public enterprises and privatise them in all sectors other than those subservient defence and security needs and sovereign functions.

The State monopolies, Government procurement and foreign companies should be subject to the Competition Law. The law should cover all consumers who purchase goods or services, regardless of the purpose for which the purchase is made.

6. World Trade Organizations (WTO): There should be necessary provision and teeth to examine and adjudicate upon anti-competition practices that may accompany or follow developments arising out of the implementation of WTO Agreements. Particularly, agreements relating to foreign investment, intellectual property rights, subsidies, countervailing duties, anti-dumping measures, sanitary and psytosanitary measures, technical barriers to trade and Government procurement need to be reckoned in the Competition Policy/Law with a view to dealing with anti-competition practices. The competition law should be made extra territorial. The statutes governing professions need to be amended to be GATT compatible.

COMPETITION

The terms "Dominance" and "Dominant Undertaking" should be defined in the Competition Law in terms of "the position of strength enjoyed by an undertaking which enables it to operate independently of competitive pressure in the relevant market and also to appreciably affect the relevant market, competitors and consumers by its actions". The definition should also be in terms of "substantial impact on the market including creating barriers to new entrants". The abuse of dominance rather than dominance needs to be frowned upon for which relevant market will be an important factor.

The predatory pricing should be treated as an abuse, only if it is indulged in by a dominant undertaking.

Exclusionary practices that create a barrier to new entrants or force existing competitors out of the market will attract the competition law. Pre-notification should be made for mergers beyond a certain limit. The Committee has suggested that the threshold limit may be fixed at the asset value of the merged entity of Rs. 500 crore or more or, the asset value of the group to which the merged entity belongs of Rs. 2,000 crore or more both linked to wholesale price index. The expression "group" as presently defined in the MRTP Act, 1969 may be adopted for the purpose of merger.

COMPETITION COMMISSION

For the implementation of the Indian Competition Act, the Commission should be established under the name of "Competition Commission of India" (CCI). CCI should be a multi-member body comprised of eminent and erudite persons of integrity and objectivity from the fields of Judiciary, Economics, Law, International Trade, Commerce, Industry, Accountancy, Public Affairs and Administration. The investigative prosecutorial and adjudicative functions will be separate.

The CCI will be the sole recipient of all complaints against infringement of the Indian Competition Act from any source whatsoever be it, it may be an ordinary citizen, business firm or any other entity including the Central and the State Governments. There will be no *suo motu* powers for the Director General to initiate any action of investigation. He will only investigate cases referred to him by the Competition Commission.

There will be collegian for choosing the chairperson and the members of the CCI. The chairperson can be from any of the disciplines listed above and should be an eminent person who has considerable exposure and knowledge in international trade, commerce and complicated issues relating to trade. For the chairperson, the maximum age limit may be fixed at seventy years and for the members sixty-five years. The terms of the chairperson and members of the CCI may be five years at a time. The chairperson will hold the rank and be entitled to the pay and perquisites of a Judge of the Supreme Court and the members, those of a judge of the High Court. The Government can remove them from the office only with the concurrence of the Supreme Court. A Code of Ethics needs to be stipulated for observance by them.

The headquarter of the CCI may be located in a city outside Delhi with permanent benches at Delhi, Calcutta, Mumbai and Chennai with further benches to be decided by the Government from time to time.

Two members of the CCI will constitute the mergers commission. CCI will have not less than 10 members including the chairperson. The headquarters will have one bench of two members as mergers commission. It will also have another bench of two members to deal with competition matters. All the other three metropolitan cities will have one bench of two members each to deal with the competition matters, in addition to the headquarters bench.

MRTP ACT

It is suggested that:

The MRTP Act, 1969 may be repealed and the MRTP Commission wound up. The provisions relating to unfair trade practices need not figure in the Indian Competition Act as they are presently covered by the Consumer Protection Act, 1986.

The pending UTP cases in the MRTP Commission may be transferred to the concerned consumer Courts under the Consumer Protection Act, 1986. The pending MTP and RTP Cases in MRTP Commission may be taken up for adjudication by the CCI from the stages they are in.

The much-awaited Competition Bill, 2001 was introduced by the Government in the Lok Sabha on Monday. The Bill aims at repealing the Monopolies & Restrictive Trade Practices (MRTP) Act, 1969 and dissolution of the MRTP Commission.

The Bill, tabled by the Minister for Law, Justice and Company Affairs, Mr. Arun Jaitley, also seeks to curb negative aspects of competition through the medium of a quasi-judicial body to be called Competition Commission of India (CCI).

The Competition Bill, 2001 seeks to ensure fair competition in India by prohibiting trade practices, which cause appreciable adverse effect on competition in markets within India. The CCI would undertake competition advocacy for creating awareness and imparting training on competition issues.

15. FOREIGN INVESTMENT AND COLLABORATION AGREEMENTS

Most countries have been making use of foreign capital to accelerate the pace of their economic growth. Even an advanced country is assisted by foreign capital or technology. India is a developing country and the importance of foreign capital and technology needs no emphasis. The domestic savings available for investment being small, foreign capital can help in augmenting the productive capacity of the country.

ROLE OF FOREIGN CAPITAL

The Role of foreign capital can easily be understood from the following points.

Economic growth

Economic growth is a function of capital formation. In the developing countries, the per capita Income and savings rate being very low, domestic capital formation is inadequate to finance the rapid economic development. Hence domestic resources may be supplemented with foreign capital to achieve the critical minimum investment to break the vicious circle of low income - low savings - low Investment - low income'.

Imports

Another way in which foreign capital helps is by facilitating the import of the items required to implement development programmes like capital goods, know-how, raw materials and other inputs and even consumer goods which may not be indigenously available. Further the demand spurt created by large scale investments may necessitate the import of consumer goods. When export earnings are insufficient to finance such vital imports, foreign capital will help in reducing the foreign exchange gap.

Exports

Foreign investments may also help to increase country's exports and reduce the import requirements, if such investments take place in export oriented import competing industries.

Gerald Meier observes that, from the stand point of national economic benefit, the essence of the case for encouraging an in flow of capital is that the increase in real income resulting from the act of investment is greater that the resultant increase in the income of the investor. If the value added to output by foreign capital is greater than the amount appropriated by investor, social returns exceed private returns.

BENEFITS

As long as foreign investment raises productivity and this increase is not wholly appropriated by the investor, the product must be shared with others, and there must be some direct benefits to other income groups as mentioned below.

Domestic labour

Domestic labour may get higher real wages because of the increase in productivity. There may also be an expansion in employment opportunities.

Consumers

Of foreign investment is cost reducing in a particular industry, consumers of the product may gain from lower product prices. If the investment is product - improving or product -innovating, consumers benefit from better quality products or new products.

Government

The increase in production and foreign trade resulting from foreign capital may increase the fiscal revenue of the Government.

External Economics

Foreign Capital may bring in a number of indirect gains through the realisation of external economies. For instance, if foreign investment is used for the development of infrastructure, this would stimulate domestic investment in industrial and other sectors.

PRIVATE FOREIGN CAPITAL

Private foreign capital generally takes the form of direct investment. The important advantages of foreign direct investment are as follows.

1. It helps in increasing the investment level and thereby the income and employment in the host country.
2. Direct foreign investment facilitates transfer of technology to the recipient country.
3. It may inspire managerial revolution in the recipient country through professional management and the employment of highly sophisticated management techniques.
4. Foreign capital may enable the country to increase its exports and reduce its import requirements.
5. Foreign investments may stimulate domestic enterprise because, to support their own operations, the foreign investors may encourage and assist domestic suppliers and consuming industries.
6. Foreign investment may also help in increasing competition and break domestic monopolies.

LIMITATIONS AND DANGERS OF FOREIGN CAPITAL

Foreign capital both private and official (Governmental and Institutional) has certain limitations. Certain additional risks are associated with foreign capital.

One of the important limitations of the utilisation of foreign capital is the absorptive capacity of the recipient country i.e. the capacity of the country to utilise foreign capital effectively. Lack of infrastructural facilities, technical know-how, personnel, inputs, market, projects feasibility, inefficiency or inadequacy of administrative machinery etc. are important factors that effect the absorptive capacity.

Sometimes, the recipient country may be pressurised to fall in line with the ideology or directions of the donor.

PRIVATE FOREIGN CAPITAL—CRITICISM

The following criticism has been levelled against private foreign capital:

1. Private foreign capital tends to flow to high profit areas rather than to priority sectors.
2. The technologies brought in by the foreign investor may not be adapted to the consumption heeds, the size of the domestic market, resource availabilities, the stage of the development of the economy etc.
3. Through their power and flexibility multi-national corporations can evade or undermine economic autonomy and control, and their activities may be inimical to the national interest of particular countries.
4. Foreign investments,, sometimes, have an unfavourable effect on the balance of payments of a country. The drain of foreign exchange by way of royalty, dividend etc., is greater than the investment by the foreign concerns.
5. Foreign capital sometimes interferes in national politics.
6. Foreign investors sometimes engage in unfair and unethical trade practices.

16. GOVERNMENT POLICY ON FOREIGN COLLABORATION AGREEMENTS

Government Policy

The Government of India's policy on foreign private investment is based mainly on the approach adopted in 1949. The basic policy is to welcome foreign private investment on a selective basis in areas advantageous to the Indian economy. The conditions under which foreign capital is welcomed are as follows:

a) All undertakings (Indian or foreign) have to confirm to the general requirements of the Government's Industrial Policy.
b) Foreign enterprises are to be treated at par with their Indian counterparts.
c) Foreign enterprises would have the freedom to remit profits and repatriate capital, subject to foreign exchange considerations.

The Industrial Policy 1991, is based on the view that while freeing Indian Industry from official controls, opportunities for promoting foreign investments in India should also be fully exploited. It is felt that foreign investment would bring attendant advantages of technology transfer, marketing expertise, introduction of modern managerial techniques and new possibilities for promotion of exports.

The ***salient features of the policy***, which would assist in achieving such an objective are outlined below: -

(i) Approval will be given for direct foreign investment upto 51% foreign equity in 36 high priority industries. There shall be no bottlenecks of any kind in this process. Such clearance will be available if foreign equity covers the foreign exchange requirement for imported capital goods. Consequential amendments to the Foreign Exchange Regulation Act, (1973) have been carried out.

(ii) Other Foreign equity proposals, including proposals involving 51% foreign equity which do not meet the criteria in para (i) above, will continue to need prior clearance. Foreign equity proposals now need not necessarily be accompanied by foreign technology agreements.

(iii) To provide access to international markets, majority foreign equity holding upto 51% equity will be allowed in trading companies which are primarily engaged in export activities and such trading houses shall be at par with domestic trading and export houses in accordance with the import-export Policy.

(iv) A special empowered investment promotion board has been constituted to negotiate with a number of large international firms and approve direct foreign investment in select areas. This special programme is aimed to attract substantial investment that would provide access to high technology and world markets.

(v) Recently, in a major initiative taken by the Government of India, in the field of capital market, a new scheme is introduced in India, which will make foreign investment in stock market easier.

This scheme allows foreign institutional investors (FII's) to invest in securities trade in the primary and secondary markets, including the equity & other securities listed or to be listed on the stock exchanges in India as also Over The Counter Exchange of India (OTCEI). FII's include institutions such as pension funds, mutual funds, investment trusts, asset management companies, nominee companies and incorporated portfolio managers. The securities include shares, debentures, warrants and the schemes floated by domestic mutual funds.

(vi) To consolidate the reforms and to give a fillip to the liberalisation process, the Government of India has by an act of Parliament amended the Foreign Exchange Regulation Act, 1973 (FERA). This act substantially diluted its regulatory provisions and brought it in line with the new liberalised industrial, trade and exchange rate policies.

The amendment has re moved a large number of restrictions on companies with more than 40% nonresident equity, removed FERA controls of Indian firms setting up joint ventures abroad and allowed Indians to hold immovable property abroad, subject to certain conditions to be stipulated by the RBI.

These changes pertain to facility extended to FERA companies on the appointment of technical and management advisor, opening of branches, acquisition of immovable property by FERA companies in India, borrowing of money or acceptance of deposits by them etc. Facilities were also extended to nonresident Indians (NRI's), Indian companies and residents for opening of foreign currency accounts in India following the introduction of partial convertibility on the current account.

Notifications were issued exempting NRI's returning to the country from declaring their assets abroad on their arrival in India and also exempting from the requirement of prior approval for acquisition of immovable property in India. All these changes are now incorporated in the amendment.

The amendment has two sets of legislative changes. Firstly, it deletes Sections 11, 12, 13, 17, 20, 21, 23, 27 and 32 of FERA as they have lost their relevance over a period of time. Secondly, it rationalises other FERA Sections, and introduces necessary amendments to them.

(vii) Foreign companies are now permitted to open branch offices in India. These can be for the purpose of representing the parent company or another foreign company in India, conducting research, undertaking export and import trading activities as well as for promoting possible technical and financial collaborations between Indian and foreign companies.

Government control over disinvestment of equity by foreign investors has been relaxed and such disinvestment is now permitted at market price for listed shares. Reserve Bank of India approval is required for the disinvestment price of unlisted shares.

(viii) The liberalised foreign investment policy is complemented by the new trade policy. The main aim of the policy is to enhance the competitiveness of the Indian economy and globalise India's foreign trade by providing greater transparency and a vastly simplified procedural framework. In addition, licensing requirements for industrial inputs have been removed, allowing free access to capital goods, raw materials, spares, components and other items.

(ix) Other important features of the trade policy are— Import and export of all industrial inputs is freely permitted, except for a limited Negative List of Imports.

- Capital goods are no longer in the Negative List of Imports. Even used capital goods can be imported subject to certain conditions.
- Import duties have been reduced significantly and range from 0 to 85 per cent. Most capital goods attract a tariff of 20 -40 per cent.
- A number of special incentives are provided to exporters.

AREAS OF FOREIGN COLLABORATION

The Government of India issues from time to time a list of industries indicating 'where foreign investments may be permitted". The lists so issued are illustrative only. No doubt, a broad technology base has been made in the country, yet a need to update the production technology may arise due to constant technological advancements in the developed countries. The Government of India (Foreign Investment Promotion Board) also considers import of technology in Industries listed in Annexure III of the Industrial Policy, in which foreign investments and technical collaborations are freely allowed.

Equity Participation

An approval for foreign participation is now available upto 51% on an automatic basis. The exceptional case exists where special expertise, skill of facilities has been developed which are not readily available indigenously.

Where significant contribution is made to exports, foreign holdings can be higher, even upto 100 per cent.

The equity participation is to be justified having regard to factors like priority of the industry, the nature of the technology involved, whether it will enable or promote exports, which may not otherwise take place and the alternative terms available for securing the same or similar technology transfer. As stated above Foreign equity participation is now allowed upto 51%, with the possibility of a higher percentage according to the proposal.

In projects where imported capital goods are required, automatic clearance will be given:

(a) in cases where foreign exchange availability is ensured through foreign equity, or
(b) if the CIF value of imported capital goods required is less than 25 per cent of total value (net of taxes) of plant and equipment, upto a maximum value of Rs. 2 crore (US$ 476,000).

In other cases, imports of capital goods will require clearance from the Secretariat for Industrial Approvals (SIA) in the Department of Industrial Development according to availability of foreign exchange resources.

In January 1998 the Government of India has further liberalised foreign direct investment by dispensing with the requirement of prior approval of the Reserve Bank of India in cases covered by automatic approval scheme. In all such cases the shares can be issued to the foreigner and foreign companies without the prior approval the Reserve Bank of India. Now certain information needs to be furnished to the Reserve Bank of India after the issue of the shares.

17. NON-RESIDENT INVESTMENTS

Investments in India by non-residents of Indian origin are known as non-resident investments. These investments have assumed greater importance in recent years.

The Government has offered a number of facilities and incentives to lure non-resident investments. It has constituted a special approval committees under the chairmanship of the secretary, Department of industrial development. The committee will decide and monitor the progress of all applications received from non-resident Indians for industrial investments involving:

a) Industrial licenses/registration/permission
b) Foreign collaborations, and
c) Import of Capital goods.

NON-RESIDENT - MEANING

For the purpose of providing facilities and incentives for investment, a non-resident of Indian origin may be:

a) An Indian citizen who has made his permanent home outside India, or who has proceeded abroad for employment or other gainful occupation; or
b) An Indian citizen who has made his permanent home outside India and acquired foreign citizenship or who is a descendant of an Indian who had earlier migrated from undivided India.

The foreign born wife of such a person is also treated as a non-resident of Indian origin.

IMPORTANCE OF NON-RESIDENT INVESTMENTS IN INDIA

There has been a tremendous growth in the bank deposits of non-residents. Till October 1, 1983 non-resident investments in India in industries amounted to Rs, 124 crore. The number of industrial ventures in India with the collaboration of non-resident Indians increased from one in 1981 to eleven in 1982 and twenty in 1983. In the first half of 1984, as many as 24 such ventures were approved. This shows the increasing importance of non-resident investments in India. The Government of India also established an organisation called *The Indian investments centre* which acts as a focal point for assistance to non-residents of Indian origin. The *activities* of this organisation are as follows:

1. It supplies comprehensive 'information on investment policies, facilities, opportunities and incentives.
2. It identifies suitable projects.
3. It brings out regularly special folders and publications relating to non-residents of Indian origin.
4. It helps in filling up and submitting application forms and keeps track of them with the concern departments to obtain expeditions approvals.
5. It maintains a liaison with the Central Government, State Governments, financial institutions and other departments to speed up the implementation of projects,
6. It organises seminars and conferences in India and overseas to appraise non-residents of Indian origin of the latest schemes.

TAX CONCESSIONS

The following tax concessions are offered for non-resident investments:

1. Dividend income from units purchased out of funds remitted from abroad or from non-resident external account, is free of income tax.
2. Balances held in non-resident external accounts in India are free from wealth tax.

3. Moneys and value of assets brought into India at the time of return to India for permanent settlement are exempt from wealth tax for a period of seven years. The value of assets acquired out of the moneys brought into India will also be exempt from wealth tax.
4. Investment in new equity issues of companies in the priority sector is free from wealth tax.
5. Investment in certain notified certificates, including 13 per cent 6 year National Saving Certificates is free from income, wealth and gift taxes.
6. Gifts made to relatives out of non-resident external accounts in India are free of gift tax.
7. Remittances to India out of foreign incomes are exempt from income tax.

These tax concessions are now available to all non-residents of Indian origin. They do not have to fulfil the test of a non-resident under the income tax Act as was necessary earlier.

Foreign exchange system in India

The central government in India has wide powers to control transactions in foreign exchange. Until 1992 all foreign investments in India and the repatriation of foreign capital required prior approval of the government. The Foreign-Exchange Regulation Act, which governs foreign investment, rarely allowed foreign majority holdings. However, a new foreign investment policy announced in July 1991 prescribed automatic approval for foreign investments in thirty-four industries designated high priority, up to an equity limit of 51 percent. Initially the government required that a company's automatic approval must rely on matching exports and dividend repatriation, but in May 1992 this requirement was lifted, except for low-priority sectors. *In 1994 foreign and nonresident Indian investors were allowed to repatriate not only their profits but also their capital.* Indian exporters are also free to use their export earnings as they see fit. However, Indian nationals only permit transfer of capital abroad in special circumstances, such as emigration. Foreign exchange in India is automatically made available for imports for which import licenses are issued.

Because foreign-exchange transactions in India are so tightly controlled, Indian authorities are able to manage the exchange rate, and from 1975 to 1992 the rupee was tied to a trade-weighted basket of currencies. In February 1992, the government began moves to make the rupee convertible, and in March 1993 a single floating exchange rate was implemented. In July 1995, Rs. 31.81 were worth US $1, compared with Rs. 7.86 in 1980, Rs. 12.37 in 1985, and Rs. 17.50 in 1990.

18. ENTREPRENEURSHIP

The term entrepreneur was introduced by a writer named Cantillon. Entrepreneur is the founder of any organisation, whether it is a big one or small one. Without an entrepreneur it is impossible to start any firm or organisation.

DEFINITION

Cantillon defined entrepreneur "as the agent who purchases means of production in order to combine them to produce a product to sell at prices that are uncertain at the moment at which he commits himself to his cost".

Though Adam Smith, Ricardo and Marx thought differently, many physiocrats accepted the above definition. It is interesting to note that the influence of Cantillon upon Adam Smith was considerable.

Prank H. Knight emphasized the assumption of risk and uncertainty as the main function of entrepreneur.

TYPES OF ENTREPRENEURS

On the basis of the degree of innovative zeal, propensity to introduce change and qualities of leadership displayed, entrepreneurs have been classified by Danhof into four distinct types.

Innovating entrepreneurship

It is aggressive in experimentation and always ready for putting attractive possibilities into practice.

Imitative entrepreneurship

It is distinguished by the preparedness to adopt successful innovations initiated by the innovating entrepreneurs.

Fabin entrepreneurship

It is characterised by great caution and skepticism, which introduces changes only when the non-introduction leads to loss.

Drone entrepreneurship

It is characterised by refusal to try new methods even at the risk of loss.

SUPPLY OF ENTREPRENEURSHIP

Supply of entrepreneurship in a country depends on several factors. The importance changes from country to country. Hence, it is impossible to say the supply of entrepreneurship applicable to all countries. However most entrepreneurs had certain common characteristics. They are:

1. To identify the opportunities for profit
2. To keep an eye for the possibility of now products
3. To observe the supply of unexploited raw materials
4. To ascertain untapped markets

5. To show willingness to take considerable risk
6. To have vision, drive and initiative
7. To devote the whole energies completely to attain the objectives.

In the early stages most of the entrepreneurs used to manage their enterprises through ploughing back of profits. But afterwards, technological as well as organisational changes favoured the growth of corporate enterprises.

Lamb in his study of Indian Business Communities, identified that the country is suffering from a variety of social obstacles for a person to rise in socio-economic status.

In developing countries economic environment as well as social barriers seem to stand in the way of entrepreneurial growth. The supply, performance and growth of entrepreneurship mainly depends on socio-psychological as well as economic factors. Let us review the existing theories of entrepreneurship to throw light on these different aspects relating to entrepreneurship.

THEORIES OF ENTREPRENEURSHIP

Economic theory did not provide for any special role to the entrepreneur. Hence, theory on entrepreneurship became necessary. In the words of Habakkuk.

" These entrepreneurs are of course not to be considered only as the cause of economic development, they are also a product, a consequence of economic development....... The entrepreneur is not a deus ex-machine; he is part of a complicated social process".

The following are some of the important theories of entrepreneurship propounded by Schumpeter. Max Weber, Hagon, Cochran, Young, Kunkel and McClelland.

Schumpeter's theory

The Schumpeterian theory of entrepreneurship is an integral part of his theory of development. Development in his sense implies carrying out of new combinations. This concept of new combinations covers the following five aspects:

i) Introduction of a good, which is not yet familiar to the consumers and also a new quality of good.
ii) Introduction of a new method of production.
iii) Opening of a new market, which means the market must be new to the product whether it is in existence already or not.
iv) Ascertainment of new sources of raw materials or half manufactured goods, irrespective of whether this source already exists or it has first to be created.
v) Carrying of new organisation should be to create or breaking up of a monopoly position.

Schumpeter called the persons who carry the above new combinations as entrepreneurs.

Max Weber's theory

The Central feature of the Weberian theory of social change consists in his treatment of the protestant ethic and the spirit of capitalism.

In the Weberian system the entrepreneurial energies are generated by following exogenously supplied religious belief i.e. protestant ethic. For people who believe in this ethic, hard work In their walks of life is not only to enable them to have their worldly desires met but also to have their spiritual needs satisfied.

Everett E. Hagen's theory

Hagen attempted to formulate a theory of social change which explains how a traditional society becomes one in which continuing technical progress takes place. The theory, instead of suggesting the key factor as the generator of social change, presents a general model of society which considers interrelationships among physical environments, social structure, personality and culture. He supports the idea of economic growth occurs interwoven with political and social change. He also rejects the notion that the solution to economic under development lies in imitating western technology. In his view, transplantation of technology into a different socio-cultural set up may not deliver the goods.

Thomas Cochran's theory

It is a sociological theory of entrepreneurial supply. According to Cochran an entrepreneur is neither a super-normal individual nor a deviant person but represents a society's model personality. He opines that the fundamental problems of economic development are non-economic. He emphasises cultural values, role expectations and social sanctions as the key elements that determine the supply of entrepreneurs.

Frank Young's theory

Young deals with the deficiencies of psychogenic mediation model, before elaborating a macro sociological interpretation of entrepreneurship. In his opinion entrepreneur does not work single handed. Entrepreneur's activity is mutually reinforcing and co-ordinated by a coherent outlook on the world. Young claims that many entrepreneurial functions are implied in his concept of solidarity. This solidarity of entrepreneurial group also avoids many economic problems that crop up in the case of an individual entrepreneur.

John H. Kunkel's theory

Kunkel's theory is a behavioural model. It starts with the premise that man's internal state is beyond the scope of presently available means of measurement and objective analysis, and knowledge of it is largely unnecessary for the explanation and prediction of behaviour.

According to the behavioural model, individual's activities are both deliberate and accidental. This approach does not deny the existence of man's internal state or depreciate human spirit. It simply does not make use of these concepts in analysis of behaviour because their ambiguities so far outweigh and advantages that their use cannot at present be justified.

David C. McClelland's theory

McClelland is concerned with the economic growth and the factors that influence it. He wanted to know the internal factors such as human values and motives that lead man to exploit opportunities, to take advantage of favourable trade conditions.

After research and analysis 'need for achievement' is considered to be the chief among the several inner motives. According to him, a desire to do well, not so much for the sake of social recognition of prestige, but for the sake of an inner feeling of personal accomplishment. In his opinion entrepreneurs display the following characteristics:

i) They do not work harder at routine tasks.

ii) They avoid gambling situation and depend on their skills.

iii) They show interest in finding out results of their decisions.

iv) They prefer to work hand at tasks that involve a real challenge which imply only a moderate risk.

Harbison on Entrepreneurship

Harbison did .not propound any theory pertaining to supply of entrepreneurship. But he made very interesting observations concerning entrepreneurship as a factor in economic development.

He suggests that entrepreneurship should be treated as a resource which has both qualitative attributes and quantitative dimensions. He categories the functions of moderate entrepreneurship as follows:

i) managing of risk in economic uncertainty,
ii) planning and innovation,
iii) Co-ordination/administration and control,
iv) routine supervision.

In small enterprises these different functions will be performed by a single individual. But in big organisations it is not possible. Therefore, Harbison characterises all the persons who perform entrepreneurial functions as 'managerial resources'. In his opinion, the effectiveness of business organisations require dynamic and innovative entrepreneurs.

Hoslitz's hypothesis

Hoslitz formulated the following hypothesis pertaining to supply of entrepreneurship.

'Marginal men, because of their ambiguous position from a cultural or social stand point, are peculiarly suited to make creative adjustments in situations of change and in the course of this adjustment process to develop genuine innovations in social behaviour.

CONCLUSION

The theories on entrepreneurship are summarised above give prominence to either sociological or psychological factors, a determinants of supply of entrepreneurship. Peter Kilby characterises theories of Schumpeter, McClelland, Hagen and Kunkel as psychological and those of Weber, Cochran and Young as sociological.

19. PROGRAMMES AND POLICIES FOR PROMPTING INDUSTRIAL ENTREPRENEURSHIP

Economic development of a country mainly depends on industrial development. For industrial development, Government should encourage the entrepreneurs through its programmes and policies.

In a developing nation like India, where population is high and incomes are low, it is inevitable to develop the small industry sector which absorbs more men with low capital. Further more, the augmentation of entrepreneurial supply 'in many regions of the country is possible only through the development of small industry sector which is considered a 'seedbed' for growth of entrepreneurship.

POLICIES PERTAINING TO SMALL SCALE INDUSTRY

Because of the importance of small industry sector in the Indian economy, let us concentrate on Government's policies for promoting entrepreneurship in this sector.

Registration of Small Scale Units

Small Scale Sector is a free sector as such entrepreneurs in this sector are not normally required to obtain a license either from the Central Government or the State Government for setting up units in any part of the country. But, small units engaged in leather and industries require licenses. However, small units are expected to adhere to the rules and regulations framed by the state and local authorities under the Factories Act, Town Planning Act etc. The small scale units are expected to get themselves registered with the Directorate of Industries of the state in their own interest. This registration, which is purely voluntary, helps the small units to get different types of assistance from the Department of Industries under the State Aid to Industries Act, medium and long term loans from State Financial Corporation and the State Bank of India and other Commercial banks, machinery on hire purchase basis from the National Small Industries Corporation etc. The registration also helps the small entrepreneurs in obtaining controlled and imported raw materials, electric power connection, accommodation in Industrial Estates, training facilities for workers of the units indifferent training institutions etc.

Organisational set up

The Industrial Policy Resolution 1956, emphasised the need for small industry development. For the development of small industrial visits through out the country, both Central and State Governments established many organisations and institutions. The following is the brief discussion about them.

National level bodies

The following are the national level-bodies established by central Government.

Small Scale Industries Development Organisation (SSIDO)

For the development of Small Scale Industries through out the country. Central Government established this organisation in the year 1954 under the Ministry of Commerce and Industry. It maintains a close liaison with the state Governments and different organisation and institutions at the national and state levels concerned with the development of small industries. It functions through 10 Directorates, 16 Small Industry Service Institutes, 7 Branch Institutes and 55 Extension centres.

Co-ordination, industrial development and industrial extension service are the main functions of this organisation.

National Small Industries Corporation (NSIC)

The NSIC was set up by the Government of India in February 1955 as a private limited company wholly owned by the Central Government.

Providing modern machines on hire-purchase basis, assisting small enterprises to participate in the store purchase programme, developing small units as ancillary units, arranging markets for small industries' products, distribution of basic raw materials through its raw material depots, import and distribution of components and parts to specific industries are the main functions of this corporation. Many of the small units in the country are utilising the services of this organisation. For example, during 1969-70, 15,000 units were benefited under hire-purchase Scheme.

Small Industry Extension Training Institute (SIETI)

The institute was set up in 1962 mainly for training officers of the Government of India, who are engaged in administering its industrial programmes. Since the year 1966 the institute has been holding international training programmes under the programme of small industry promotion in developing economies. It is also bring out a number of useful publications relating to the problems of small industries.

Small Industries Development Book of India (SIDBI):

The Small Industries Development Book of India is the apex bank for small scale industries. It extends assistance to SSI units through various schemes. The activities of SIDBI are as under:

i) imitating steps for technology upgradation and modernisation of existing units,

ii) expanding the channels for marketing the products of SSI sector in domestic and overseas markets,

iii) promotion of employment oriented industries especially in semi-urban areas to create more employment opportunities and thereby checking migration of population to urban and cosmopolitan areas.

The other promotional agencies at the national level are Industrial Development Bank of India (IDBI), Industrial Finance Corporation of India (IFCI), Industrial Credit and Investment Corporation of India (ICICI), Khadi and Village Industries Commission (K & VIC), Council of Scientific and Industrial Research (CSIR), India Investment Centre (IIC). National Boards for Developing Handicrafts, coir, silk etc.

State level Bodies

Small industry development is primarily the responsibility of State Governments. The following are the various industry promoting agencies working in the states.

Directorate of Industries

The Director of Industries, who is the head of the State Directorate is assisted at the headquarters by a group of technical and administrative personnel. The Director is incharge of subjects relating to industries which include large and small scale industries, handicrafts etc. At the district level, generally, an assistant director is incharge of the programme who is assisted by a number of inspectors. At block level an extension officer looks after the extension work associated with the small industry promotion.

Small Scale Industrial Development Corporations

These Corporations were established to assist entrepreneurs in setting up small units. Today, they offers a comprehensive range of entrepreneurial services. The main objectives of the corporations are to aid, counsel, assist, finance, protect and promote the interests of small scale industries in the respective states.

The main activities of the corporations can be broadly classified into the following categories:

a) Promotion and developmental activities that stimulate further growth of industries,
b) Procurement and supply of scarce raw materials to small scale industries,
c) Revival of sick units, and
d) Management of the production units under its own control.

The corporations offer technical consultancy services, prepares feasibility reports free of cost, conducts the district-wise survey of industries, participates in risk capital through its joint venture scheme or margin money assistance scheme. The corporations have started hire purchase schemes under which they supply machinery on hire purchase basis to educated unemployed under itself employment scheme.

Industrial Infrastructure Corporations

These Corporations provide industrial infrastructure and thereby help the development of small, medium and large industries in the State.

To identify potential growth centres, to acquire land for Industrial Development Areas (IDA) and Industrial Estates (IEs), to establish IDAs and IEs equipped with roads, water, power supply and also to build worksbeds and develop plots etc. are the objectives of these corporations.

State Financial Corporations

These Corporations in the states mainly grant medium and long term loans to small and medium industries for purchase of plant and machinery etc. These are state based autonomous institutions.

Institutions set-up for Small Industry Development in India is as follows:

National level

1. Small Industries Development Organisation (SIDO)
   - policy formulating, coordinating and monitoring agency
2. National Small Industries Corporation (NSIC) with 5 regional offices
   - supply of machinery on hire - purchase basis
   - Registration of units for participation in the purchase programmes of the central and state governments
   - Marketing assistance - internal and external
   - Development of prototypes of machinery and equipment, and other facilities
3. Commissioner for industrial cooperatives
   - coordinations of policies for industrial cooperatives
4. Special Institute for Training and Development
   i) National Institutions of Small Industry Extension Training (NISIET), Hyderabad
   ii) National Institute for Entrepreneurship and Small Business Development (NIESBD), New Delhi
   iii) Entrepreneurship Development Institute of India (EDII), Ahmedabad, Lucknow, Patna, Bhopal—promoted by IDBI, IFCI, ICICI and SBI
   iv) Central Institute of Tool Design (CITD), Hyderabad
   v) Central Tool Room and Training Centres - Ludhiana, Delhi, Kolkata and Bangalore
   vi) Central Institute of Hand Tools (CIHT), Jalandhar - Provision of technology, raw materials, designs and testing for hand tools industry
   vii) Institute for Design of Electrical Measuring Instruments (IDEMI), Mumbai
   viii) Central Machine Tool Institute, Bangalore
   ix) Central Institute for Plastics Engineering and Tools - Chennai, Ahmedabad

x) National Institute of Foundry and Forge Technology, Ranchi.

State Level

1) Directorate of Industries with a network of District Industries Centres at the district level, industries officers at the sub-division level and extension officers at the block level.
   - Registration of Small Scale units
   - Raw material quota
   - Import quota
   - Financial assistance under the State Aided to Industries Act.
   - Industrial Estate
   - Technical Consultancy
   - Training of entrepreneurs
   - Industries Cooperatives
   - Compilation of Statistics
   - Overall administration of the village and small industry sector
2) Small Industry Development Corporation
   - Supply of scarce raw materials through raw material depot
   - Machinery on hire purchase
   - Marketing assistance
   - joint ventures in the small scale sector
   - Entrepreneurship development
   - Trade Centres
   - Industrial Estates
3) Industrial Infrastructure Cooperation
   - Industrial Area Development Board/ Authority
   - Plans and develops industrial estates and industrial areas
4) Industrial Development Corporation
   - Promotion of industrial units in the medium and large-scale including joint and public sector ventures

   - Planning and development of industrial estates and industrial areas
   5) Industrial Investment Finance Corporation
   - Finances medium and large units up to a certain investment ceiling with direct participation in share capital and under writes new issues
6) Agro Industries Corporation
   - Supply of agricultural machinery/equipment on hire
   - Development of agro-based industries
   - Sale of agro-inputs like fertilizers and pesticides
7) Electronics Development Corporation
   - Promotion of industries in the field of electronics including joint sector and public sector projects
8) Leather Industry Development Corporation and other similar Commodity Corporations
   - Development of specific types of village and tiny sector units relating to a particular trade
9) Rural Industries Marketing Corporation
   - Marketing of village industry products and provision of a variety of services needed by village and tiny units
10) Industrial and Technical Consultancy Organisations (Sponsored by IDBI/ IFCI/ICICI)
   - Technical Consultancy Services to small and medium scale projects.

POLICIES PERTAINING TO LARGE SCALE INDUSTRY

Here, the objective regarding large scale industry is not to survey the strategies of industrial development adopted by the Government, but only to examine the measures taken by the Government to encourage entrepreneurship with particular reference to licensing policies.

The industrial policy statement of 1948 was the first formal enunciation of Government's policy views in respect of ensuring industrial development of the country on sound lines. To implement the industrial/policy resolution, the Industries (Development and Regulation) Act, 1951 .was passed.

The important provisions of the act are:

a) A license from the Central Government is needed for establishing a now industrial unit.
b) Government can initiate investigations into certain specified industries.
c) Government can take over management of undertakings which fail to carry out its instructions for improvements in management.
d) the act also empowers the Government to prescribe prices, methods and the volume of production and channels of distribution.

The provisions of the act were applicable to scheduled industries. Although the initial list of scheduled industries contained only 42 major industries, the list was considerably expanded in the year 1956 and later. Thus entrepreneurs faced many problems in getting licenses from the Government.

RECENT DEVELOPMENTS

To get licenses for large industry the entrepreneurs used to submit many number of papers and wait for a long time. In the year 1990 to reduce the troubles of the entrepreneurs, the Janata Dal Government came with a new proposal of De-licensing policy.

The Congress Government in its new industrial policy, 1991 took a radical step and declared that no license is required to start any industry. This is of course not applicable to the 18 major industries listed by the Government. This de-licensing policy is mainly meant for facilitating and encouraging the entrepreneurs to come forward and start new industries.

20. JOINT SECTOR

Joint sector concept is not new to India. The concept was, for the first time, initiated by the Government under the Industrial Policy Resolution 1956. In simple term, joint sector is an extension of mixed economy. In mixed economy, both private and public sectors exist. Public sector is owned and managed by the Government and the private sector, though owned and managed by private parties but it is controlled by the Government in public interest. But in joint sector, the two, the Government and the business houses are in partnership. The sector is owned and managed jointly by the Government and the business houses. It combines the entrepreneurial initiative of private business firms with the social philosophy of the public sector. The concept of joint sector is based on the philosophy that the Government can easily invest the funds in an enterprise and the business houses can operate the venture efficiently. If these two are mixed, there would be a marvellous progress in the industrial field of the country.

DEFINITIONS

There is a controversy over the definition of 'Joint Sector'. According to Dutt Committee (1969) the joint sector would have three concepts.

a) "Existing private enterprises belonging to large industrial houses should be brought under the joint sector by public financial institutions converting their loans into equity".
b) "The Joint Sector would include those industrial units in which both public and private investment had already taken place and - - - here the state has already been taking an active part in direction and control".
c) "large sized industrial units in Schedule 'B' and 'C' categories - - - - necessitated on account of technical

and economic advantages of large scale, should necessarily be in the Joint Sector to prevent concentration of economic power. In this case, the joint sector should be treated as belonging to the public sector- - - -".

J.R.D. Tata, in a memorandum submitted to the Government suggested "A joint sector enterprise is intended to be a form of partnership between the private sector and the Government in which state participation of capital will be not less than 25 per cent, the day to day management will normally be in the hands of the private sector partner, and control and supervision will be exercised by a board of directors on which Government is adequately represented".

The definition given by Dutt Committee is in favour of public sector, whereas Tata's definition tilts in favour of private sector. The important aspect in the context of joint sector is concerning the ownership and management.

JOINT SECTOR - ADVANTAGES

The following are the various advantages possessed by joint sector.

1) Because of ownership and management and control over the enterprise, both the Government and the private sector will contribute to the industrial development of the country.
2) Joint sector may provide social control over big industrial houses without nationalisation.
3) Under joint sector autonomy and managerial efficiency of private sector and the accountability and the attainment of social objectives of public sector may be attained.
4) The financial requirements may be fulfilled very easily with the co-operation of both the sectors.
5) There will be proper check on the concentration of economic power and monopolistic tendencies, prevalent in private sector.

6) There will be an overall growth in economic and social fields. Interests of various parties like consumers, shareholders, Government and dealers would be protected.

Thus, the concept of joint sector would benefit the economy in every field. The charge of inefficiency, generally, levelled against the public sector would be washed away under joint sector. In this sector, the investment of public funds would be less, management would be better and the social objectives would be attained easily.

JOINT SECTOR—GOVERNMENT POLICY

The Government made its policy towards joint sector clear only in the Industrial policy statement of 1970, under which heavy industries and consumers industries were to set up in joint sector. The financial institutions, for the development of joint sector, were given the right of converting loans into equity.

The Industrial Policy statement of 1973, made the position of joint sector clear as follows :

1. Industries in which the entry for big industrial houses and foreign companies have been prohibited may be allowed under joint sector.
2. In joint sector enterprises, the Government will actively participate in matters relating to decision making, management and operation.
3. Each joint sector enterprise will be set up taking the economic and social objective of the Government.
4. The Government will act as a promoter for new and middle level entrepreneurs.

The Government made the guidelines for the purpose of joint sector specifying the share of each type of investor. The *equity participation* of various parties will be as follows:

Sector/Interest	*Only domestic industries*	*Collaboration between domestic and foreign industries*
1. Government	26% of paid up share capital	25% of paid up share capital holding holding
2. Private sector	25% "	20% "
3. Public and financial institutions	49% „	35% „
4. Foreign aid		20% "

Regarding *management,* a mixed pattern has emerged. The operational decision making rests with the managing director and his team of managers while the policy decision making rests with the board of directors.

Thus joint sector has filled wall into our professed philosophy of mixed economy, public control and public accountability. It is a compromise between the total state monopoly and complete private autonomy. It is motivated by considerations of growth and social Justice. A few plants established in joint sector are the Cochin Refinery, Madras Refinery, Gujarat Fertilisers, Madras Fertilisers. Some more plants established with foreign collaboration are the Heavy Electricals Limited, Bhilai Stool Plant etc.

21. CONCEPT AND FUNCTIONS OF ENTREPRENEURSHIP

Concept: The word 'Entrepreneurship' appeared first, in French according to Encyclopaedia Britannica in the early 16th Century, it was applied to those who were engaged in Military expedition. In the 17th Century, it was extended to cover civil engineering activities such as construction fortification. Oxford English Dictionary (1897) defined entrepreneur simply as "the director or manager, of a public musical institution; one who 'gets up' entertainments, especially musical performance. Not until its supplement appeared in 1933, did the dictionary recognise that the word has a place in business, and would mean "one who undertakes an enterprise especially contractor—acting as intermediary between capital and labour". Joseph Schempeter noted that the fifteenth century thinkers had established ideas about the businessman and his functions. But it was only in the beginning of the 18th Century that the word was used to refer to economic activities.

French economist Richard Cantillon was the first to introduce the term 'entrepreneur'. However, it was John Mill who popularised its use among English speaking Economists.

There has been faced a definitional problem concerning entrepreneur. Like other economic concepts, entrepreneurship has long been debated. It has been used in various ways and various senses. Even today it is not clear, as to what does this term exactly mean, and that who should precisely be called an entrepreneur. A manager is sometimes described as an entrepreneur, sometimes an innovator or a capitalist and sometimes all of them combined into one refer to an entrepreneur.

Earlier Concept

In the beginning the attitude of the classical economists was very cold towards the use of this term or towards its role in economic theory. Building writes that "in classical economics the firm is a shadowy entity, and the entrepreneurs even shadowier. . . . .or at least shady when is not shadowy".

Adam Smith, though greatly influenced by the physio-crats and by Cantillon, gave little importance to the entrepreneurial activities of leading and directing in his analytic scheme of the economic process. He did not use the word entrepreneur but instead repeatedly talked about the employer, the master, the merchant, and the undertaker. He seems to be of the opinion thus capitalist economy ran of itself, by what is popularly known as the "Invisible hand" in conditions of Laissez Faire.

From Cantillon to Marshall Entrepreneurial concept was treated in the same manner and elevated entrepreneurship to the fourth factor of production, though this function was identified by different names. Nothing was done on the supply side of this factor of production. Moreover all these economists considered entrepreneurship in the context of stationary equilibrium but all of them failed to recognise it as a force in economic development.

Cantillon defined entrepreneur as "an agent who buys means of production at certain prices in order to combine them into a product that he is going to sell at prices that are uncertain at the moment at which he commits himself to his cost."

Say and Marshall put entrepreneur in the centre of both the productive and distributive theory and stressed on the aspect of co-ordination and organisation. According to J.B. Say. "the entrepreneur is the economic agent who unites all means of production—the labour of the one, the capital or the land of the other and who finds in the value of products which result from their employment, reconstitution of the entire capital that he utilises and the value of the wages, the interest and the rent which he pays as well as profits belonging to himself".

Schumpeter played with the word innovations and emphasised innovation as the function of an entrepreneur. Schumpeter's entrepreneur is a highly specialised concern. Innovations may occur in the following form:

1. Introduction of new goods;
2. The use of a new method of production;
3. The opening of a new market;
4. The conquest of a new source of supply of raw materials; and
5. The reorganization of any industry.

Entrepreneurial Functions

An analysis of the conceptualization of the process of the development of entrepreneurship as envisaged by the different economists, one can briefly list out the possible functions usually carried out by the entrepreneurs. These are as follows:

1. Planning the project
2. Organisation
3. Risk bearing
4. Management
5. Uncertainty bearing
6. Innovation

1. *Planning* is the first step in the direction of setting up of an enterprise. To make his conception to work he plans out the complete setting to be adopted, i.e., ,
   a) selection of product line;
   b) determination of the form of organisation (individual or partnership, or corporate, or some other form) ;
   c) estimation of the capital needed;
   d) selecting the location;
   e) selection of the capital resources;
   f) studying the government regulations, and selecting the ways to fulfil the formalities; and
   g) studying the type of market and market strategy to be adopted.

   The blue-print of the proposed project, prepared by the entrepreneurs, enlists all these details in a formal systematic format. It is formally submitted to the authorities concerned for obtaining the legal sanction for the venture.

2. *Organization* implies the co-ordination of the various factors active during the promotion stage, and at the performance story or otherwise of an enterprise largely depends on the efficiency of the organisational network employed and monitored by the entrepreneur.
3. *Risk-bearing* as a function of entrepreneurship refers to the use of capital fixed or variable, by the entrepreneur against the payment of a fixed rate of interest. It does exist in the business irrespective of the fact whether the entrepreneur is successful or not.
4. The management here stands for not only the working of the venture but also the tackling of the day-to-day problems. It includes control and direction of men and machinery most efficiently in the short run, along with the planning and forecasting its future expansion and the policies in the long run.
5. *Uncertainty-bearing* refers to the uncertain trend of the markets. It includes the trade credits also.
6. *Innovation* implies "doing of new things or doing of things that are already being done in a new way". That is introducing new fields of technology in the production. Thus, it is the creation of new markets, discovery of new and better sources of raw-material, and finally the creation of monopoly or the breaking up of it.

Besides the above functions, the entrepreneur has to perform many other activities at the later stage, e.g.,

a) Diversification of production.
b) Expansion of the enterprise.
c) Co-ordination with outside agencies (like suppliers, customers, financial agencies, government organisations, etc.).

d) Cordial employer-employee relations.
e) Tackling labour problems.
f) Keeping in touch with new policies and programmes of the land.
g) Helping the venture by participating in the local industrial associations.

At the initial stage the functions are mostly performed by the entrepreneurs all by themselves. Latter, as the enterprise grows, the number of employees also grows, and the need for highly trained and skilled labour arises. The problems of relations with labour, labour unions, suppliers, customers, government become more complex. At this stage it becomes necessary to delegate a number of decisions to the subordinates. But as the powers delegated are of a routine nature, his central functions remain those of decision making, capital structure, diversification and relations with the outside agencies, etc. Arthur H. Cole has described the entrepreneur as a decision maker.

1) The determination of the business objectives of the enterprise and the change of those objectives as conditions require or make advantageous;
2) The development of an organisation including efficient with subordinates and all employees;
3) The securing of adequate financial resources, the relations with existing and potential investors;
4) The requisition of efficient technology equipment and the revision of it as now machinery appears;
5) The development of a market for the products and the devising of now products to meet or anticipate consumers demand; and
6) The maintenance of good relations with the public authorities and with society at large.

While interpreting the views expressed by different economists in context of the underdeveloped countries the functional analysis of the entrepreneurs becomes complex, since he has to perform a host of other activities, against the odds. As in the advanced capitalist countries he cannot be merely a 'promoter', everywhere.

The functions of an entrepreneur with reference to the undeveloped countries include a wide range of activities, say "In underdeveloped countries the functions of a given person in entrepreneurial capacity include innovation, promotion, capital and labour".

An extensive sketch of the potential-scope of the entrepreneurial task in an underdeveloped economy had been provided by Kilby:

1. Perception of market opportunities (novel or imitative).
2. Gaining command over scarce resources.
3. Purchasing inputs.
4. Marketing of the product and responding to competition.
5. Dealing with the public bureaucracy (concessions, licences, taxes).
6. Management of human relations within the firm.
7. Management of customers and supplies relations.
8. Financial Management.
9. Production Management (control by written records, supervision, co-ordinating input flows with orders maintenance)
10. Acquiring and overseeing assembly of the factory.
11. Industrial engineering (minimising inputs with a given production process).
12. Upgrading processes and product quality.
13. Introduction of new products.

Though these can be delegated but it depends upon the scale of production, social factors, and entrepreneur's self-efficiency. In an underdeveloped country an entrepreneur lacks the help of the markets for components, materials, labour, capital markets (which have already standardised products and trained workers). He also lacks the communications network, i.e., specialised industrial newspapers, magazines, and statistics of the complete structure of the industry collected by the government, and other institutions, which provide all the information in the developed countries, say about the sources and availabilities of inputs, nearest and the best possible outlets for outputs.

22. ENTREPRENEURSHIP AND ECONOMIC DEVELOPMENT

The industrial entrepreneurship is the vital force in industrialization and economic development. Development and Growth of Entrepreneurship is directly related to the economic development of particular region. In the broadest sense economic development is influenced by, and its basis revolves around, industrialization, i.e., the correlation exists.

IMPORTANCE OF ENTREPRENEURSHIP IN ECONOMIC DEVELOPMENT

The Human Factor is studied with considerable importance and interest, since the development of all the sectors of the economy is determined by the human resources. The entire change and development of the civilization is surely the result of industrialisation, which was made possible by none other but the entrepreneur. McClelland has rightly hypothesized that the need for achievement, i.e., the entrepreneurial potential is the psychological factor which engenders economic growth and decline. The sense of high achievement and motivation introduced by the entrepreneurs brings about the required necessities in a class of society which transform the perception of the economic thinking, which is necessary to bring about the economic development.

The economists who have discussed this aspect of economic development require the simultaneous transformation of a society to exhibit western social structure and even to assume most of the social values of the West. Whether the transplantation of the western social structure and the values is desirable or not, the fact remains that the discussion of the problems of the present-day developing economies is perforce to be based on the past development experience of the western societies with necessary caution because of socio cultural differences among countries.

Arthur Cole suggests that to study the businessman is to study the main figure in economic activity. Michael Palmer says that a reason such as Cole's consequences might ensure from such a study. As a possible answer, he feels that there appears to be some correlation between economic growth and business formations. Secondly, important to the formation of a business is the activity of an entrepreneur. Thirdly, certain areas may possess capital and resources while scarce from the viewpoint of entrepreneurs. Hence, in these areas the pace of economic development is not up to the expected levels. In other areas, where numerous entrepreneurs exist along with an adequate resource base, we might expect a flourish of economic activity. In the words of Rostow the behaviour pattern of people relevant for economic development can be summed up in six propensities, the propensity to develop fundamental science; to apply science to economic ends; to accept the possibilities of innovation; to seek material advance; to consume; and to have children. Kuznets highlights the role of human resources when he said, The major capital stock of an industrially advanced nation is not its physical equipment; it is the body of knowledge amassed from tested findings and discoveries of empirical science and the capacity and training of its population to use this knowledge effectively. Jan Tinbergin has suggested *five human qualities* which are conducive to economic development.

a) an interest in material well-being,
b) an interest in techniques, and in innovation,
c) an ability to look ahead, and a willingness to take risks,
d) perseverance, and
e) an ability to collaborate with other people and to observe certain rules.

"It is easy to see that these five qualities are necessary for various reasons-the first because this provides a motive, the second because so many different technical aids are used in modern industry and these are constantly being improved, the third because installation of capital goods produces results only after a considerable time, the fourth because these results may well prove disappointing and the fifth because the whole process requires continuous and harmonious co-operation if it is to work."

The irrational and superstitious views should be replaced by rational view of the world. People must learn to be goal oriented, and work to achieve the given ends. The systems of thought must be devised, like the invention of accounting by the Italians in the middle ages, which permitted a rational view of the world. Though besides the relations of an individual to his society, family, structure, class structure, ethnic factors, religion, urbanization, national character, social institutions etc., impinge an economic development.

This outlook of the behavioural-pattern of the people according to Adelman and Morris in the study of 74 countries, has been profoundly affected by the rapid expansion of urban areas, industrialisation and growing commercialisation of agriculture, and increasing exposure to modern technology. In addition, the attitudes, outlook and aspirations of the people are rapidly being transformed by the spread of education, mass communication media and contact with western ideas. These transformations have weakened traditional social organisation, and have resulted in increases in social tensions and marked political instability. Thus, among countries at the intermediate level, social structure no longer exercises as over-powering an influence upon the daily lives of the majority of the people as it does in countries at the lowest stage of development.

Till the industrial revolution, the economy was very simple, and hence it did not require or engender entrepreneurship of a high order. No doubt the functions performed by a peasant, an artisan, a feudal lord or a capitalist resembled the functions of their prototypes in the modern age.

With the introduction of science and technology, there is a growing awareness of the economic backwardness, hence there is a changed role of the entrepreneur in the developing economies. It is the Schumpeterian innovative entrepreneur who puts the science and technology in economic use. As there are no diminishing returns to technological progress, continued technological progress will, thus, result in an unbounded increase in total and per capita income. Admittedly the innovative entrepreneurs are the key to rapid industrialisation and thereby economic development. They are, however, found in developed regions only. Some doubts are already expressed about their availability in underdeveloped regions like ours.

According to Peter Kilby, there are mainly four major tasks performed by the entrepreneur, viz.,

1. Exchange relationship,
2. practical administration,

3. Management control and
4. Technology.

Those four tasks consist of:

I. Exchange Relationships:
   a) Perception of market opportunities.
   b) Gaining command over scarce resources.
   c) Purchasing inputs.
   d) Marketing of the product and responding to competition.

II. Practical Administration:
   a) Dealing with the public bureaucracy.
   b) Management of human relations within the firm.
   c) Management of customer and supplier relations.

III. Management Control:
   a) Financial Management.
   b) Production Management.

IV. Technology:
   a) Acquiring and overseeing assembling of the factory.
   b) Industrial engineering.
   c) Upgrading process and product quality.
   d) Introduction of new production techniques and products.

Decision making in the above fields is the major activity area, wherein 'the entrepreneur operates. It is also noteworthy that this is a very complex area of activity requiring him to work under the uncertain conditions. An entrepreneur works under the particular conditions of uncertainty pertaining to pricing (Cantillon), innovating (Schumpeter), promoting ideas into business operations (Dewing), determining the type of business (Evans) and making decisions under alternative choices (Danhof) or changing market conditions (Evans).

Thus, entrepreneur within this proposed framework, would involve (i) a determination of the types, and degrees of uncertainty confronting the performance of a particular, operation and (ii) the ability to make the appropriate decisions, necessary for the goal attainment.

The conclusion drawn by Kilby from the evidence is that, "entrepreneurial performance in those roles involving 'exchange relationships' and 'political administration' is vigorous and effective." On the other hand, entrepreneurs typically do not apply themselves with equal intensity or skill to their tasks in the realms of management control and technology. Deficiencies in these latter areas represent in many instances the operational bottlenecks to indigenous industrial development.

It is only in the recent years that the role of entrepreneur has been considered of very great significance in shaping the industrial growth and economic development in both the developed and underdeveloped countries. The economic history of the presently developed countries, for example, America, Russia and Japan tends to support this fact. In fact, the crucial role displayed by the entrepreneurs in the development of western countries has made the people of underdeveloped countries too much conscious of the significance of entrepreneurship for economic development. Now, people have begun to realise that for achieving the goal of economic development, it is necessary to increase entrepreneurship both quantitatively and qualitatively in the country. It is the only active and enthusiastic entrepreneurs, who fully explore the potentialities of the country's available resources-labour technology and capital. That is why the significance of their role for economic development is recognized by several economists in various ways. For example, Schumpeter, as noted earlier, visualized the entrepreneur as the key figure in economic development because of his role in introducing innovations.

Parsons and Smelser describe entrepreneurship as one of the two necessary conditions for economic development, the other being the increased input of capital. Harbison includes entrepreneurs among the prime movers of innovation, and 'Sayigh simply describes entrepreneurship as a necessary dynamic force. Meir and Baldwin held, "development does not occur spontaneously as a natural consequence when economic conditions are in some sense right a catalyst or agent is needed, and this requires an entrepreneurial activity."

From the opportunity conditions point of view, the underdeveloped regions due to the paucity of funds, lack of skilled labour and non-existence of a minimum social and economic overheads,: are less conductive to the emergence particularly of innovative entrepreneurs, in these regions, non-innovative entrepreneurs, namely, imitators, Fabian and drone are noticed, however. In such regions, entrepreneurship does not emerge out of industrial background with well developed institutions to support and encourage it. Therefore, the entrepreneur in such region may not be an "innovator" but an "imitator" who would copy the innovations introduced by the "innovative" entrepreneurs of the developed regions. In these areas, according to McClelland's concept of personality aspect of entrepreneurship, some people with high achievement motivation come forward to behave in an entrepreneurial way to change the stationary inertia, as they would not be satisfied with the present status that they have in the society.

Decision making under uncertainties is, therefore, key to development. The evidence that follows from the analysis proves the point that industrial development, and' the socio-economic development are, to a large extent, dependent on the entrepreneurial activity, which in turn, depends upon the process of decision making, particularly under the conditions of uncertainty. Basically in terms of socio-economic development, it may safely be concluded that it is the entrepreneur, who introduces sciences and technology to the field of management studies. Such an intermingling of the different branches of learning; not only speeds up the process of economic development, rather it introduces the realistic transformation of the social thinking.

23. RISKS INVOLVED WITH ENTREPRENEURSHIP

Entrepreneurship involves four types of risks

a) Personal risks.
b) Financial Risks.
c) Know-how Risks.
d) Vested-interest Risks.

a) **Personal Risks:** The individual deciding to become an industrial or a business entrepreneur has to be prepared to sink or swim in the career he has chosen. There are heavy opportunity costs involved. Besides, industry ownership involves physical hardships, and the emotional strain in an irregular, though sometimes attractive income. The entrepreneur often has to deny himself the pleasures attached to family and social life, also.

b) **Financial Risks:** While there are possibilities of getting a good return and sometimes very attractive returns on the capital invested, there is also the risk of business failure which may drive the entrepreneur into bankruptcy. The impact in the latter case would be particularly hard if the person has put all his life's savings in the business, and he has nothing else to feed back upon. On the other hand, if he has borrowed money from the banking and financial institutions, then he is hopelessly under the burden of debt.

c) **Know-How Risks:** This is the vital risk involved in entering the business or industry, particularly without adequate preparations in terms of knowledge and skill. Two broad types of know-how required for success are: technical and mechanical. The industry owner should have the know-how in at least one of these.

d) **Vested-interest Risks:** New entrepreneur may find the existence of direct or indirect vested interest-groups who may take steps to ruin his prospects.

Therefore, the scheme of entrepreneurial promotion need to be accepted as a matter of risk priority. The whole process thus, goes through closely interrelated stages, but the sequence to be followed may vary according to particular situations; say stimulation identification, technical guidance, promotion, follow-up and, of course, maintenance and development.